Building a
WORDPRESS
BLOG
People Want to Read

Second Edition

SCOTT MCNULTY

Building a WordPress Blog People Want to Read, Second Edition
Scott McNulty

Peachpit Press
1249 Eighth Street
Berkeley, CA 94710
510/524-2178
510/524-2221 (fax)

Find us on the Web at: www.peachpit.com
To report errors, please send a note to errata@peachpit.com

Peachpit Press is a division of Pearson Education.
Copyright © 2011 by Scott McNulty

Executive editor: Clifford Colby
Editor: Kathy Simpson
Production editor: Danielle Foster
Compositor: Danielle Foster
Indexer: Ann Rogers
Cover design: Charlene Charles-Will
Interior design: WolfsonDesign

ISBN-13: 978-0-321-74957-4
ISBN-10:   0-321-74957-X

9 8 7 6 5 4 3 2 1

Printed and bound in the United States of America

To Marisa, my wife, who lovingly supports me in whatever I do (well, other than when I don't clean up after myself).

About the Author

If it supports blogging, chances are that Scott McNulty has used it. He owns more e-readers than one man should and more books than are sensible.

Scott lives in Philadelphia with his wife, Marisa. By day, he works at The Wharton School of the University of Pennsylvania, and by night, he blogs about whatever strikes his fancy at http://blog.blankbaby. com. He has also been known to tweet once or twice under the handle @blankbaby.

Acknowledgments

Another book written by little old me but made possible by the work of many talented people. Thanks, as always, to Cliff Colby for continuing to believe that I am at least an adequate writer. Special thanks to Kathy Simpson, who once again managed to make me look good despite my best efforts. Danielle Foster and indexer Ann Rogers created another beautiful book, and for that, I thank them.

Finally, thanks to everyone who has read anything I've written in my life. Nothing makes authors happier than knowing that somewhere out there, people are reading our words.

Contents

1

Why WordPress?

Everyone from Martha Stewart to Fortune 500 companies to your 12-year-old niece seems to be blogging nowadays. Blogging has gone from something only the nerdly found themselves doing a few years ago to something that your mother likely knows about—if she isn't doing it herself.

WordPress has done its part to help spread the allure of blogging by making it very easy to start a blog—and to update that blog after it's up and running. WordPress isn't the only blogging tool in town, though. Lots of popular tools are out there, including Movable Type, Tumblr, Habari, and Blogger. Given all these choices, why should you use WordPress?

Check the following sections for the good and the bad about WordPress. To get it out of the way, I start with the bad.

The Downside of WordPress

All is not sunshine and fruit punch in the world of WordPress. Using a blogging platform that is engineered like this one has a couple of drawbacks:

- **Appeal to bad guys.** Popularity and an open code base are generally a good combination, but a few people out there are always looking to ruin everyone's fun. Because WordPress runs so many high-profile sites, some nefarious types are on the lookout for flaws that can be exploited. Luckily, the WordPress developers are very quick to patch vulnerabilities, but you have to stay on top of the releases.

- **Dynamic page generation.** WordPress dynamically generates most of the pages that you see. Each time you load a post, a bunch of things are happening in the background: Database queries are fired off, PHP code is executed, and then the page is displayed. Usually, this system isn't a problem; it ensures that the content of your blog is as up to date as possible. But this approach is a little more resource-intensive than a static approach and can translate to your blog's being unavailable under heavy load.

note   Movable Type, the other blogging heavyweight, takes the opposite approach. Movable Type (MT for short) stores posts, comments, and the like in a database just like WordPress does, but it creates static HTML pages from that data. This arrangement makes MT a little leaner when serving up content, but publishing a post can take more time because each index page needs to be rebuilt. MT has added an option to use a dynamic system, but by default, it publishes static pages.

The Upside of WordPress

Remember when you were a kid, and you asked your mom if you could do something all the other kids were doing? She replied, "If everyone else jumped off a bridge, would you jump off too?" Despite the fact that my friends weren't known bridge-jumpers, the advice is clear: Be your own person, and you'll be better off in life.

That advice works well as a general life practice, but when you're considering a blogging platform, you want to pick the one that has the most users. Why? Because along with all those users comes some pretty neat stuff, such as an active developer community, a wide range of reference materials, and a large base of people you can turn to for help.

WordPress has all those features in spades. Many of today's most popular blogs—including TechCrunch, ICanHasCheezburger.com, and *The New York Times'* blogs—are powered by WordPress, so you can rest assured that WordPress is capable of handling the traffic generated by your adoring audience.

Furthermore, WordPress can be extended by little bits of code called *plug-ins,* which I talk about in detail in Chapter 14. Created by members of the WordPress community, plug-ins are often available for free or for a small fee. These plug-ins can make WordPress do all sorts of things it isn't able to do out of the box.

The active plug-in developer community owes its existence in large part to the fact that WordPress is distributed under the GNU General Public License. This license means two things:

- WordPress is free.

- You're allowed to alter the code to suit your needs and share your modified code with anyone, so long as you distribute it under the same license (for free and in such a way that others can change your code and share it as well).

WordPress.com vs. WordPress.org

Now that I've convinced you that WordPress is the way to go, you have another choice to make: self-hosting or hosted version?

Hosting your blog on WordPress.com

WordPress.com (**Figure 1.1**) hosts WordPress blogs for free. Hosting your blog on WordPress.com frees you from having to get your own hosting space and making sure that your Web server has the software that WordPress needs to run. It also means that your blog is ready for traffic spikes associated with popular posts. The team behind WordPress.com takes care of all the back-end stuff (patching servers, upgrading software, and the like) and leaves the blogging to you.

Figure 1.1 The WordPress.com logo.

Keep a few things in mind when you host your blog on WordPress.com:

- **WordPress URL.** The URL of your blog will be something like www.*mygreatblog*.wordpress.com. If you're going to host a blog for professional reasons, you may not want to advertise the fact that you're using a free service.

- **Extra cost for advanced features.** WordPress.com offers some advanced features such as domain mapping, which allows you to point any domain to a blog hosted on WordPress.com (getting around the amateurish URL), but you have to pay for these features.

- **No access to code.** Given the nature of WordPress.com, you have no access to your blog's code. You can't modify the way your theme looks without paying a little extra, and you can't upload your own custom theme.

  Remember those cool plug-ins I mentioned earlier in this chapter? WordPress.com offers a bunch of them for your use, but you can't upload your own plug-ins, so if you're interested in using one that isn't available on WordPress.com, you're out of luck.

note You can use your own plug-ins when you buy a VIP WordPress.com package, which starts at $600 a month. If this blog is your first one, however, I don't recommend going that route.

WordPress.com is a great option if you're looking to get into blogging with WordPress but don't want to make a big commitment. Registering is free and easy, and you'll be up and blogging in no time.

This book concentrates on the other option: hosting your own installation of WordPress. That being said, much of the content of this book (especially the chapters about posts, pages, and links) is valid for both blogs hosted on WordPress.com and self-hosted blogs.

Hosting your own installation of WordPress

Your other option is downloading the WordPress code from WordPress.org (**Figure 1.2**) and installing it yourself. Because you're hosting the blog yourself, you decide what plug-ins you'll use, and you have complete control of all the files. What's more, pointing a domain to your installation won't cost you anything extra (above and beyond your Web-hosting bill and registration fees, that is).

Figure 1.2 The WordPress.org logo.

This option gives you the most control of your blog, but it does come at a price: You're responsible for everything. You have to maintain backups of your blog and make sure that your blog is ready for a sudden surge in traffic, and you won't have anyone but yourself to blame if you screw something up.

Hosting your own installation of WordPress won't be much of a challenge if you've maintained a Web site before. If you're new to Web hosting, you'll have a learning curve (but you have this book to help you!).

New in WordPress 3.0

One of the challenges a tech author faces when writing about something like WordPress is change. Those pesky developers are always at work improving WordPress. This book covers WordPress 3.0.1, the most current version as of this writing.

WordPress 3.0 introduces several new features and sports a radically different look from WordPress 2.6 (which the first edition of this book covered). Among the new things covered in this edition are the updated user interface, easier plug-in and theme installation, custom post types, and the new default theme.

2

Installing WordPress

The famed 5-minute installation is one of the most-talked-about aspects of WordPress. I've installed WordPress several times (a good thing, because I'm writing a book about it), and the process has always been painless, but knowing a few things will make it much smoother for those who are new to WordPress.

The most common way to install WordPress involves using a remote *server*—a computer that's set up to serve Web sites to anyone who wants to visit them. I concentrate on this option for most of the book.

You can also do what is known as a *local install* of WordPress by using your own computer as a local server. This installation isn't accessible to other folks but is good for testing. I won't be covering local installs in this book, however.

Getting What You Need

In this chapter, I walk you through installing WordPress on a remote server. First, though, you need to gather some files and tools, and double-check some settings. WordPress requires certain programs to be available on your remote server, and to access that remote server from your computer, you need an FTP client.

A Web host

You need to have Web-hosting space before you can install WordPress. Picking a hosting company is a topic that could fill a book in and of itself. But here are a few things to look for in a host, because your host has to have them for you to run WordPress:

- **PHP version 4.3 or later.** WordPress itself is written in PHP, so it makes sense that PHP has to be installed on the server for WordPress to run.

- **MySQL version 4.0 or later.** MySQL is an open-source database that stores all sorts of information for your WordPress install. All your posts, users, and settings will be stored in this database. (I cover setting up the MySQL database later in the chapter.)

Local tools

When your Web hosting is all set, you need to make sure that you have the necessary tools on your local machine to set up WordPress. Here's the list:

- **FTP client.** You need to get files from your computer to your hosting space. You have several ways to transfer files, but the easiest is *FTP* (geek talk for *File Transfer Protocol*). FTP isn't a program, but an agreed-upon protocol that programs use to transfer files. File-transfer programs that use the FTP protocol—called *FTP clients*—are available for every operating system. For more information, see the nearby "FTP Clients" sidebar.

- **A text editor.** The WordPress application is made up of files that you can edit with any plain old text editor. (Windows users can use Notepad, for example; Mac OS X users can use TextEdit.) Before you use your FTP client to upload files to your hosting space, you need to use a text editor to edit a configuration file (see "Editing the wp-config File" later in this chapter).

note **Any text editor will do the trick, but don't use Microsoft Word. Word adds a bunch of stuff to text files that only causes trouble with WordPress files.**

FTP Clients

Chances are that you're using either of two operating systems (OSes) on your computer: Apple's Mac OS X or a flavor of Microsoft Windows. Both OSes have command-line FTP tools built into them, but I'm a graphical-interface kind of guy. Here are some FTP clients that you should check out.

For Windows:

- **FileZilla.** FileZilla (http://filezilla-project.org) is free; open-source; and available for Windows, Mac, and Linux computers. You can't beat that!

- **WS_FTP.** WS_FTP (www.ipswitchft.com) has been around forever. Both the Home and Professional versions are feature-packed—as they should be, because pricing starts at $39.95 for the Home version.

For Mac OS X (my OS of choice):

- **Cyberduck.** Cyberduck (http://cyberduck.ch) is open-source and full-featured. And who doesn't like ducks?

- **Transmit.** Transmit (www.panic.com/transmit) is the gold standard of FTP clients for the Mac and is made by a great indie Mac developer (Panic). For $29.95, you get one license for this well-thought-out FTP client.

The WordPress code

After you've gathered all your tools, you need the raw materials: the WordPress files. Getting these files couldn't be easier. Simply point your browser to www.wordpress.org/download. You'll see a large blue oval that's a link for downloading the most current and stable version of WordPress, which is WordPress 3.0.1 at this writing (**Figure 2.1**).

Figure 2.1 The WordPress download page. See that big blue oval? That's where you can snag your own copy of the WordPress code.

Notice that I said the blue oval links to the *stable* version of WordPress. If you like living on the edge, you can check out the Beta Releases and Nightly Builds links on the left side of the page.

Beta Releases

The word *beta* should be familiar to anyone who's used the Web in the past few years. A *beta release* of a product allows the public to use that product before it's fully done. When you use a beta release, you get in on the snazzy new features ahead of the rest of the population, and the company gets an unpaid tester to encounter any nasty bugs that may be lurking in the not-ready-for-prime-time code.

What Are Those Files, Anyway?

You've downloaded and uncompressed the latest version of WordPress, and now you have a folder called wordpress sitting on your computer. A quick peek inside the folder reveals a bunch of other files and folders. Not too impressive, is it?

Sorry if you were expecting more, but that handful of files is going to enable you to share your thoughts (and cat pictures) with the entire world. That's pretty powerful stuff, wouldn't you say?

At this point, you can ignore most of the files in the wordpress folder. You may want to check out the read-me file (though this book is far more entertaining), and if you're curious, you can open any of the files in your favorite text editor. Just make sure not to change any of the code, because changes could lead to unexpected behavior in your install.

You can join the WordPress beta program by signing up on the tester list— but if you're new to WordPress, you shouldn't sign up unless you're a fan of the "sink or swim" learning methodology.

Nightly Builds

Nightly builds often are even scarier than betas. WordPress is a large open-source project, which means that an army of people out there are using their free time to work on the code that powers WordPress. When a creator is done with the code, he or she checks it into the system for someone else to look over. After all the changes have been given a once-over, a *nightly build* is created, containing all the most recent, untested changes.

I suggest downloading a nightly build of WordPress only if you're the type of person who has to be on the bleeding edge. If you buy your cell phone from eBay Japan just so you can have it a few weeks before your friends do, the nightlies may be up your alley.

note WordPress.org maintains an archive of old WP releases, just in case you're hankering for some olde-tyme WordPress. Point your browser to http://wordpress.org/download/release-archive/ for a trip down memory lane. Be warned, however, that many of these releases were superseded by new releases that fixed security issues. Download at your own risk.

Setting up the MySQL Database

It's almost time to install WordPress, but first, you need to create a MySQL database for WordPress to store all your content and user accounts. The installation will fail if you don't set this database up beforehand.

The specifics of setting up a MySQL database vary greatly from hosting company to hosting company. That being said, it's still worth your while to go through the process of creating a MySQL database.

 note Keep in mind that these exact directions will work only for the hosting company I use—DreamHost (www.dreamhost.com)— but the basics can be applied to all hosts.

First, log into your Web host's control panel. This control panel is where you can manage any number of features of your Web-hosting account, such as billing information, domain registrations, and MySQL databases.

Look for a link that says something like *Manage MySQL Databases* (**Figure 2.2**). This link takes you to the page where you'll be creating the database for your blog.

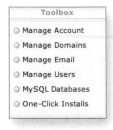

Figure 2.2 This collection of links appears in the top-left corner of DreamHost's control panel. Clicking the MySQL Databases link takes you to the MySQL management section.

At this point, you should see a form asking you for a bunch of information required to set up your very first MySQL database (**Figure 2.3**).

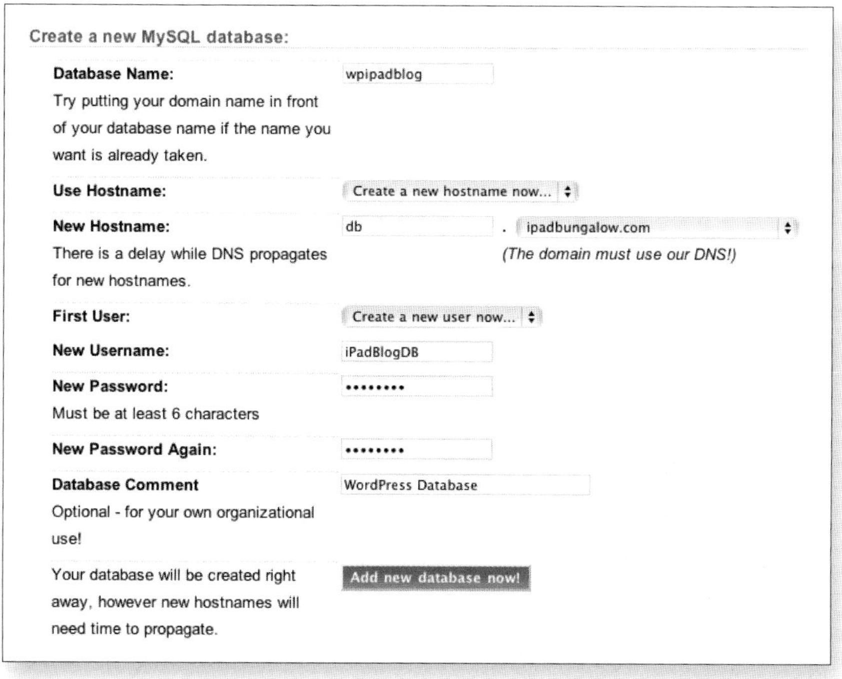

Create a new MySQL database:

Database Name: wpipadblog

Try putting your domain name in front
of your database name if the name you
want is already taken.

Use Hostname: Create a new hostname now... ▾

New Hostname: db   .   ipadbungalow.com   ▾

There is a delay while DNS propagates   *(The domain must use our DNS!)*
for new hostnames.

First User: Create a new user now... ▾

New Username: iPadBlogDB

New Password: ••••••••

Must be at least 6 characters

New Password Again: ••••••••

Database Comment   WordPress Database

Optional - for your own organizational
use!

Your database will be created right   **Add new database now!**
away, however new hostnames will
need time to propagate.

Figure 2.3 The new-database form (DreamHost's is shown here) asks you for information that any Web host will need to set up a database for you.

Some MySQL Tips

Before I delve into the ins and outs of setting up a MySQL database, here are some pointers to keep in mind:

- Name your database something that you'll remember.

- You need to create a database user that will install all the WordPress tables (a process that the install script takes care of), but don't use the same user name and password that you're going to blog with. Using a different name and password makes it a little harder for folks to guess your database credentials.

  The database user who installs WordPress needs to have full rights for the WordPress database, meaning that he or she can create—and delete—all manner of things. A good password is your best defense against malicious tomfoolery.

Here's a review of each text box shown in Figure 2.3 so that you can fill out your Web host's new-database form with confidence:

- **Database Name.** Every database needs a name, and you'll need to know what your database is called when you install WordPress. Be sure to give your database a unique name; don't name it wordpress or something equally easy to guess, which would only help people who want to break into your database for nefarious reasons. (The Internet is a great place, but you'll find some jerks out there.)

- **Hostname.** At first, you may think that a host name and a database name are the same thing. They aren't. The *host name* is the name of the server on which your database runs. As you can see in Figure 2.3, DreamHost allows you to use an existing host name or create a new one, and I've decided to create a new one for my new blog.

note You need to check with your Web-hosting service to see what your database's host name should be. Some services allow you to use the host name localhost, which means that your blog and database run on the same server.

- **First User.** Your database needs a user account so that you can use it, and much like every other account you've ever created, this account needs a user name and password. Make sure that both the user name and password are difficult to guess, but also make sure that you'll remember them, because you'll need this information to install WordPress.

- **Database Comment.** This field may or may not be available, depending on your Web host, but if it's available, I strongly suggest that you enter a descriptive comment. This comment will help you figure out which database belongs to what blog after you rack up a few WordPress blogs. (These blogs are so easy to install that I'm willing to bet you'll find yourself the happy owner of at least two more blogs than you ever thought possible.)

After you've plugged in all the information about your MySQL database—and made a note of its name, the host name, and the user information—go ahead and click the Add New Database Now button. Depending on your Web host, your database will be available immediately or after a few minutes.

 note **Your database needs to be accessible before you continue your WordPress installation; otherwise, the install will fail.**

Choosing Your Blog's URL

Before you upload the files, you have one more thing to think about: your blog's URL structure.

Suppose that you've registered the domain www.wordpressforall.com, and you plan to host your WordPress blog there. You have a few options, including these:

- If you want your blog to be the primary content of your domain, you should upload the WordPress files directly to the site's root folder. When you do, people who go directly to your URL will be greeted by your blog.

- If you plan to have a landing page or some other content living at the root of your site, you should upload the WordPress files to a subdirectory. To get to your blog, people will have to enter a URL like www.wordpressforall.com/blog. (In this example, you would create a subdirectory called blog at the root of the site and then upload all the WordPress files to that subdirectory.)

note **If you want your blog's URL to be something other than www.yourblog.com/wordpress, be sure to rename the default WordPress directory before you upload it to your site, or create the correctly named folder on your remote host and upload the WordPress files to that folder.**

Installing WordPress

Now that you've figured out your blog's structure, you're ready to install WordPress. Use your FTP client to upload your blog files to the directory you chose (refer to "Choosing Your Blog's URL" earlier in this chapter). You should see a file list something like the one shown in **Figure 2.4**.

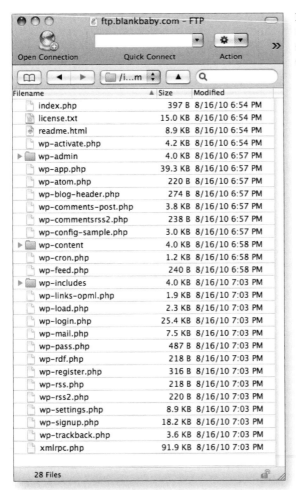

Figure 2.4 WordPress files uploaded to a remote server via the magic of Cyberduck.

After you've got all your files uploaded, the real fun begins.

Installing the software

To install the WordPress software, follow these steps:

1. Point your browser to the URL of your soon-to-be-functional blog.

    You'll be greeted by a WordPress error message (**Figure 2.5**). Worry not—this is supposed to happen. Each WordPress installation has a *configuration file,* which contains information that the WordPress install needs to function (the location of your database, the database user name and password, and the like).

Figure 2.5 Your first WordPress error! Don't worry—this error is by design.

2. Click the Create a Configuration File button to continue the installation.

 note   You can also create a configuration file by hand, which I cover in "Editing the wp-config File" later in this chapter.

You'll see a list of things that you need to set up your WordPress blog (**Figure 2.6**). As I've already mentioned, you need to have your database name, user name, password, and host. I didn't mention table prefix, but I'll cover that in a moment.

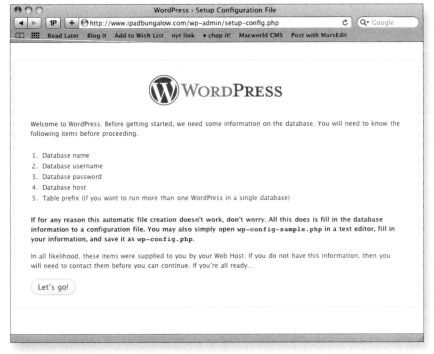

Figure 2.6 WordPress rather helpfully gives you a heads-up on the information you need to install it.

3. Click the Let's Go! button to continue the installation.

   Now you're cooking.

4. In the next screen (**Figure 2.7**), enter the information that you jotted down while creating your MySQL database (refer to "Setting up the MySQL Database" earlier in this chapter).

The final setting in this screen is called Table Prefix, and by default, it's set to wp_, but as you can see in Figure 2.7, I've changed this value. Even if you don't plan on running more than one WordPress install using the same database, I recommend that you enter a custom value here to make it more difficult for hackers to guess what your database tables are named.

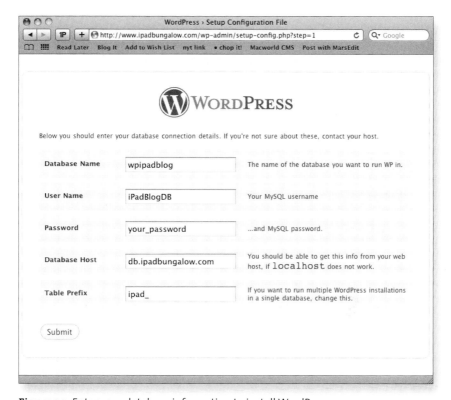

Figure 2.7 Enter your database information to install WordPress.

note Databases are made up of tables, each of which contains all the data for various parts of your blog: the posts, the comments, and so on. Each of these tables must have a unique name within the database. Other databases can have a table that shares a name with another database's table, but each table within a database must have a unique name.

5. After you've entered all your information, click the Submit button.

6. In the resulting screen (**Figure 2.8**), click the Run the Install button.

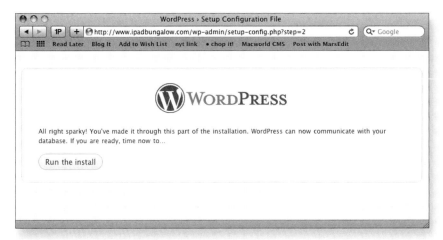

Figure 2.8 All your information has been entered, and the configuration file has been created. You're ready to install WordPress.

You go to the Welcome screen (**Figure 2.9**), where you can personalize the WordPress install a little.

7. In the Site Title text box, enter what you want your blog to be called.

If you can't think of anything great at the moment, don't worry; just enter something. You can easily change your blog's name later.

8. By default, the first user created for your blog has the user name admin, as you see in Figure 2.9, so you should change the entry in the Username text box to something that you'll remember.

 note Don't enter the user name that you'd like to use for yourself. The user that you create in this screen will have full administrative rights on your blog (which I cover in Chapter 3), so you'll want to make this user name difficult for someone to guess.

9. Enter a strong password in the appropriate text boxes.

Make sure that the password is one you'll remember, because unlike previous versions of WordPress, WordPress 3.0 doesn't display your password and won't even email it to you on request.

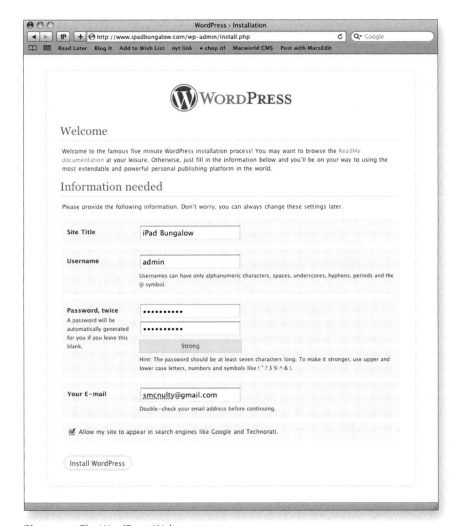

Figure 2.9 The WordPress Welcome screen.

10. Speaking of email, in the Your E-Mail text box, enter an email address that you have access to.

The install process will send this address an email containing some information about your newly installed blog.

11. Finally, clear or check the box titled Allow My Site to Appear in Search Engines Like Google and Technorati.

Not every blog is meant for public consumption, so if you don't want people to find your blog easily, clear the check box. Otherwise, leave it checked. (How are you going to get famous if no one can Google you?)

12. Click the Install WordPress button.

After a couple of seconds, you should see a Success! screen containing details about the administrator account for your new blog (**Figure 2.10**).

Figure 2.10 Success! WordPress has been installed.

Logging in for the first time

The moment you've been waiting for is finally here. Click the Log In button in the Success! screen (refer to Figure 2.10), and you're whisked away to the WordPress login screen (**Figure 2.11**), which will become familiar to you in very short order.

Figure 2.11 The login screen.

Enter the admin-account information and then click Log In. (Don't bother checking the Remember Me check box; in Chapter 3, I show you how to set up a different account that you'll use to log in to your blog in the future.)

Editing the wp-config File

As I mention earlier in this chapter, every WordPress install includes a configuration file, called wp-config.php, that stores information about your blog's database (which you entered in step 4 of "Installing the software" earlier in this chapter). You can edit this file in any text editor, if you want to check it out.

If you're code-squeamish, worry not! The file you're about to look at is honest-to-goodness PHP code, but I'm here to help you. (Also, the bits you're interested in for purposes of WordPress are well documented in the code itself.)

Look inside the wordpress folder, either on your computer or on your server, and open the file called wp-config-sample.php (which I'll call *wp-config* for short). You should see a bunch of code, along with some very helpful comments about what you should and shouldn't touch in this file.

The wp-config file has several sections, which I'll call MySQL Settings, KEY, Languages, Debugging, and "not for editing."

note **All text in the wp-config file that appears between the characters //** and **// is a comment. Comments explain the different parts of the file.**

MySQL Settings

The MySQL Settings section is how WordPress knows where to look for the MySQL database you set up earlier. All you need to do is enter some information in this file.

note **Remember to enter all your values between quotation marks; otherwise, your install will fail.**

Here's the text of this section:

```
// ** MySQL settings - You can get this info from your Web host
   ** //
/** The name of the database for WordPress */
define('DB_NAME', 'wpipadblog');
/** MySQL database username */
define('DB_USER', 'ipadblogdb');
/** MySQL database password */
define('DB_PASSWORD', 'your_password');
/** MySQL hostname */
define('DB_HOST', 'db.ipadbungalow.com');
/** Database Charset to use in creating database tables. */
define('DB_CHARSET', 'utf8');
/** The Database Collate type. Don't change this if in doubt. */
define('DB_COLLATE', '');
```

And here's what you need to fill in:

- **DB_NAME** is the name of your database. (I usually call my databases something creative like *blogname*-wp, where *blogname* is the name of the blog that I'm installing.)

- **DB_USER** and **DB_PASSWORD** are where you enter the user name and password of the MySQL database that you created.

- **DB_HOST** is the name of the computer that's running your MySQL database.

- **DB_CHARSET** and **DB_COLLATE** both have to do with the character set that your MySQL database is using. If you have no idea what that sentence means, you should leave these variables set to their defaults.

You'll notice that **TABLE_PREFIX** isn't an option here, because it isn't grouped with the other database settings. Look for the text **$table_prefix,** which will allow you to set a custom table prefix for each WordPress install.

KEY

Here's the text of the KEY section:

```
define('AUTH_KEY',         'put your unique phrase here');
define('SECURE_AUTH_KEY',  'put your unique phrase here');
define('LOGGED_IN_KEY',    'put your unique phrase here');
define('NONCE_KEY',        'put your unique phrase here');
define('AUTH_SALT',        'put your unique phrase here');
define('SECURE_AUTH_SALT', 'put your unique phrase here');
define('LOGGED_IN_SALT',   'put your unique phrase here');
define('NONCE_SALT',       'put your unique phrase here');
```

The KEY section is all about making your installation of WordPress more secure. You may be tempted to skip this section because it's optional (WordPress will work just fine if you don't assign eight unique key values here), but it's such a great way to secure your blog that it's well worth a few seconds of your time.

note **WordPress populates these values automatically if you use the Web-based install.**

What do these keys do? WordPress uses *cookies*—little files that are stored in your Web browser to remember who you are and what your login information is. A hacker could grab one of your cookies (no one likes to share cookies!) and log in to your blog posing as you. Setting these keys lets WordPress *hash* (scramble) those values to make it much harder for someone to get any information from the cookies. (He'd need to guess your hash key to unscramble the values, which is why the keys should be very complex.) These keys are also used in your MySQL database to make the passwords stored there harder to decipher.

The keys work best when they're completely random and more than 60 characters long. I have two pieces of good news that will make using these keys seem much more attractive:

- You never have to remember the values of these keys. You set them in your wp-config file once and then forget about them (though they'll be stored in the file itself, should you feel nostalgic for them).

- The smart folks behind WordPress set up a service that generates three very strong, and very random, keys for you. All you have to do is visit https://api.wordpress.org/secret-key/1.1/salt, which generates the code for you; just copy and paste that code into your wp-config file. Nothing could be easier.

Seriously, stop reading these instructions and set those keys now. I'll wait.

Done? Good! I'll move on.

Languages

The default WordPress language is English, which is great for us English-speaking bloggers. But what if you want to blog in another language? That's where `define ('WPLANG', );` comes in.

Localizing WordPress to another language requires a few steps:

1. Define `WPLANG` as the language code you want.

   You can find a full list of the codes needed to define the `WPLANG` variable as your language of choice at http://codex.wordpress.org/WordPress_in_Your_Language.

2. Create a folder called languages inside the wp-content folder of your WordPress installation folder.

3. Obtain the proper MO file for the desired language, and put it in your new language folder.

   The MO file contains all the information that WordPress needs to be displayed in anything from Italian to Portuguese. Volunteers create MO files, some of which are available at http://codex.wordpress.org/WordPress_in_Your_Language.

Debugging

If you aren't a WordPress developer, you can leave this section alone. When define('WP_DEBUG', false); is set to true, error messages give you much more detail so that you can debug various bits of your code.

"Not for editing" section

Here's the final section of the wp-config file:

```
if ( !defined('ABSPATH') )
  define('ABSPATH', dirname(__FILE__) . '/');
require_once(ABSPATH . 'wp-settings.php');
```

You shouldn't edit this section. The wp-config file acts as a repository for settings that another file—wp-settings.php—uses to do all the heavy lifting of the WordPress installation. Fiddling with this section of the file will result in installation errors, so don't touch it!

Troubleshooting Common Installation Problems

As you see, installing WordPress isn't too tough, but sometimes, bad things happen to good blogging software. A couple of common errors could happen when you're installing WordPress, and in this section, I show you how to work around them.

WordPress can't access database

Most problems occur when WordPress can't access your MySQL database. If you see an error message like the one shown in **Figure 2.12**, make the following checks and then reload the install page:

Figure 2.12 A common installation error (but an easy one to correct).

- Double-check your DB_NAME, DB_USER, and DB_PASSWORD values. An easy way to make this check is to connect to your MySQL database using something other than WordPress. (Your Web-hosting service should provide you a MySQL management tool.) If you can connect by using the values set in the wp-config file, reset the database user's password, and try again.

- Make sure that you're running the correct version of MySQL (version 4.0 or later).

PHP isn't enabled

The other common problem involves PHP and is also easy to fix. When you visit the URL to install WordPress, you may see a screenful of text starting with <?php instead of the install form. This text means that you don't have PHP enabled on your server.

Contact your Web-hosting company or system administrator to find out how to enable PHP (and make sure that you're running PHP 4.3 or later). After you enable PHP, reload the install page. All should be well.

3

Managing User Accounts

WordPress is installed and running, and you've logged in as the administrative user you created during the installation process. I bet that you think it's time to blog about something, right? Not so fast, Sparky. First things first: You need to create a user account for yourself.

Why not just use the default admin user account that was created during the installation? Many people do because it requires the least effort (we're all lazy people, when you come right down to it), but best practice is to use that admin account for administrative tasks only. That way, you don't have to do any tricks to get posts attributed to your name instead of the admin user name; all the user roles are clear from the get-go.

Managing User Profiles

The first time you log in to WordPress, you see the *Dashboard* (**Figure 3.1**), which I cover in more detail in Chapter 4. The Dashboard is the control center for your blog—the place where you access all sorts of options, statistics, and settings.

Figure 3.1 The WordPress Dashboard.

Resist the urge to click all over the Dashboard with wild abandon; instead, focus your attention on the options on the left side of the screen. This list of links is your gateway to managing all the aspects of your blog. At the moment, your first order of business is to check out the default user profile, so click Users to open the Users screen—and also reveal a few new options in a Users quick menu (**Figure 3.2**).

Figure 3.2 The Users screen, listing the user you created during installation. (By default, this user is called admin.)

When you first open this screen, it lists only one user, called admin, but all the users of your blog will be listed here eventually. You'll use this screen to add new users (which I discuss later in this chapter) and to change the profiles of existing users (which I discuss next).

Changing a user profile

You can change a user profile in either of two ways:

- **Editing yourself.** If you want to edit the account under which you're currently logged in, choose Your Profile from the Users quick menu on the left side of the Users page (refer to Figure 3.2).

- **Editing someone else.** To edit another user's information, choose that person's user name from the Users quick menu. (Not all users can do this, thanks to user roles, more on which in a bit.)

Either way, you end up at the Profile page, which has a bevy of options for you to set (**Figure 3.3**).

Figure 3.3
Profile page for the selected user.

Setting profile options

The profile options are grouped together, though I think the order of the options is a little odd. (I'd rather have the password options closer to the top of the page, for example. Something tells me that you're more likely to change your password than your user name.) In the following sections, I look at each group of options and explain what they mean.

Personal Options

You can set two visual aspects of the blog in your user profile: Visual Editor and Admin Color Scheme (**Figure 3.4**). This section also allows you to turn on keyboard shortcuts for comment moderation.

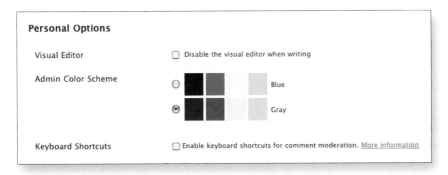

Figure 3.4 Setting the personal aspects of your blog.

Visual Editor. WordPress posts are written in HTML (Hypertext Markup Language), which is the tag-based language that Web pages are written in. Web browsers know how to interpret this code into the lovely words and images you read on people's blogs and Web sites. The only problem is that not everyone knows HTML; in fact, some people aren't interested in learning about it. They want to blog, not code. That's where the WordPress Visual Editor comes in.

The Visual Editor option turns the WordPress posting form (which I promise to talk more about in Chapter 6) into a WYSIWYG editor. A WYSIWYG (what you see is what you get) editor allows you to do things like insert links, format text, and create lists, using controls that are familiar to anyone who's ever edited a document in a word processor. The Visual Editor generates all the HTML code for you so that you can concentrate on writing that great post about your weekend.

note Why do you even have an option to turn off the Visual Editor? Before this feature was introduced in WordPress 2.0, users had to hand-code their posts, and some people still like handcrafting their HTML (and argue that they can do it faster and better than any silly old WYSIWYG editor). If you agree with them, simply check this box.

Admin Color Scheme. You have two color-scheme choices for the WordPress admin interface. The Gray option will be familiar to anyone who's used previous versions of WordPress; the Blue option is a new color scheme that's a bit ... well, bluer. WordPress doesn't give you an easy way to create your own color schemes, which is a shame, but free add-ons to WordPress called *plug-ins* let you color to your heart's content. (I cover plug-ins in Chapter 14.)

Keyboard Shortcuts. If you check this box, you'll be able to perform several operations on comments by using keyboard shortcuts. I cover all these options in Chapter 11.

 note The color schemes, as well as everything else listed in the Profile page, are applied on a per-user basis. That means that I can choose to use the Gray color scheme, and another user of the same blog can pick Blue. Everybody wins.

Name

Figure 3.5 shows the name settings for each user. WordPress is very flexible in the way it displays a user name; you just have to be sure to fill in as much information as possible to gain maximum flexibility. (WordPress can't display any information you haven't entered.)

Name

Username	admin	Usernames cannot be changed.
First Name		
Last Name		
Nickname *(required)*	admin	
Display name publicly as	admin ⬍	

Figure 3.5 The Name section.

You can set these options:

- **Username.** You can't change this setting for the admin user. This user name is the one you'll use to log in to WordPress. Like your password, it's case-sensitive.

- **First Name.** The user's first name goes in this text box (shocking, I know). This setting is optional, though filling in the text box gives you more name-display options, because WordPress won't be able to display your first name if it doesn't know what your first name is (and isn't it rude not to introduce yourself to your blog?).

- **Last Name.** The user's last name is also optional.

- **Nickname.** We're all familiar with the concept of nicknames. (In some circles, for example, I'm known as Dr. Awesome. Sure, those circles exist only in my imagination, but they still count.) The WordPress nickname option is just a name, other than user name or first name/last name, that you want to go by on your blog. You can have comments or posts credited to your nickname instead of your user name or real name.

- **Display Name Publicly As.** This setting is where that Nickname option pays off. You can choose to have your name displayed on posts and comments in a few ways: user name, first name only, last name only, first and last name, last and first name, or nickname (**Figure 3.6**). Dr. Awesome is pleased.

Figure 3.6 The available display names are based on the information provided in the Name section.

Contact Info

The Contact Info section (**Figure 3.7**) is straightforward, so I don't need to walk you through each option. Note, however, that an email address is required so that WordPress can send you notifications.

A variety of theme tweaks and plug-ins (see Chapter 13 and Chapter 14, respectively) can help you take advantage of contact information later—perhaps by displaying instant-messaging user names on comments or user pages—so fill in as much or as little of this information as you're comfortable with.

Figure 3.7 An email address is the only bit of contact info WordPress requires; the rest is just fun to have.

About Yourself

Figure 3.8 shows the "about" page for a user—you, in this case.

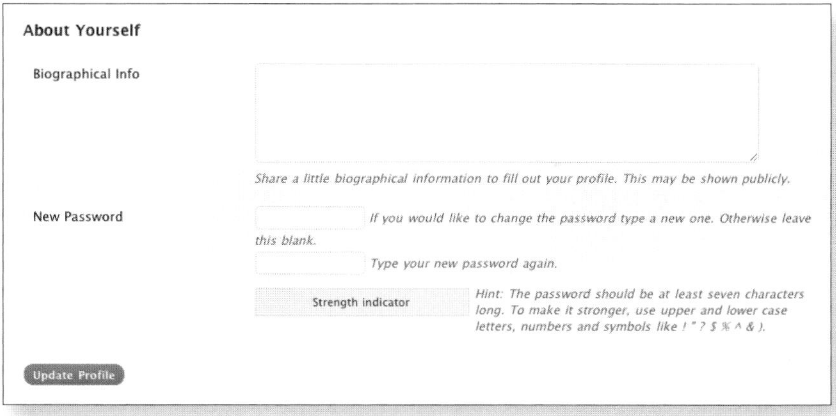

Figure 3.8 WordPress wants to know about you, but the password section is the most important part.

Providing biographical info is optional, but as the Web becomes more of a social place, it's nice to share a little bit about yourself with your readers. (Besides, who doesn't like writing about himself or herself?) The New Password section, however, is required.

Changing your WordPress password is simple: Enter your new password twice (no need to enter your old password, because you can change your password only while you're already logged in), and click Update Profile.

Clicking this button also saves the rest of the changes you made to your profile. If you want to change something in your profile but don't want to alter your password, just leave both password boxes empty. The changes to your profile will be saved, and your password will remain the same.

Notice the Strength Indicator feature below the password text boxes. This feature helps you pick a strong password but won't stop you from setting a weak password. (It'll just be disappointed in you.)

 tip The best passwords are long, complicated, and hard to guess. Don't use something common like password or your birthday. Do use a mix of letters (uppercase and lowercase), numbers, and symbols.

Adding and Deleting Users

Now that the default admin user has a strong password, you're ready to create a user account for yourself. Are you excited? You're getting so close to blogging that I can almost taste it.

Adding a new user

There are two ways to access the Add New User screen:

- Click Users on the left side of the Dashboard. The Users screen opens (refer to Figure 3.2 earlier in this chapter). Click the Add New button at the top of the screen.

- Once again, click Users on the left side of the Dashboard, and a couple of options appear in a quick menu (**Figure 3.9**). Choose Add New to add a new user.

Figure 3.9 Many of the items on the left side of the screen contain quick links, like Add New.

Both methods send you to the same place: the Add New User screen (**Figure 3.10**), where you need to fill in some information about your new user.

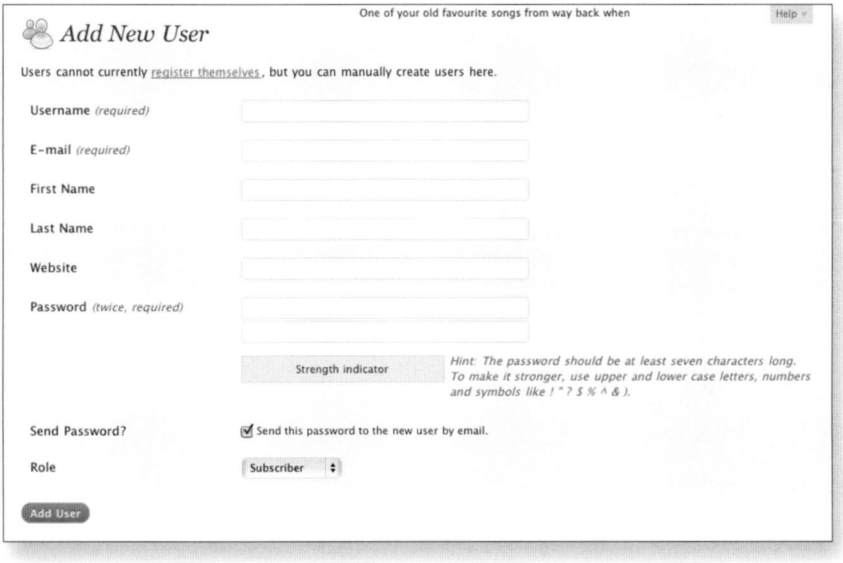

One of your old favourite songs from way back when   Help ▾

Add New User

Users cannot currently register themselves, but you can manually create users here.

Username *(required)*

E-mail *(required)*

First Name

Last Name

Website

Password *(twice, required)*

Strength indicator   Hint: The password should be at least seven characters long. To make it stronger, use upper and lower case letters, numbers and symbols like ! " ? $ % ^ &).

Send Password?   ☑ Send this password to the new user by email.

Role   Subscriber ▸

Add User

Figure 3.10 The Add New User screen.

The following information is required:

- User name

- Email address

- Password

tip **If you know the user's name and Web site, I suggest filling in that information as well, even though it's optional. The more information you share about yourself with your readers, the better they will feel they know you.**

By default, WordPress will send this newly created user an email containing his user name and password, along with the URL of the WordPress admin login page. If you'd rather not send this email, clear the Send Password? check box.

Choose a role from the Role drop-down menu (I cover your choices in the next section) and then click the Add User button. You've just created a new user for your blog.

Understanding user roles

WordPress has five user roles that you can assign to any user—one role per user. These roles define what a particular user can and can't do.

Here are the five roles, in decreasing order of power:

- Administrator
- Editor
- Author
- Contributor
- Subscriber

Each role sees, and can access, different things in WordPress's Dashboard.

In the following sections, I look at these roles and how they work in a typical blog.

Administrator

An Administrator has the power to do anything on the blog. This user can activate and deactivate plug-ins; modify themes; create and delete users; set global blog preferences; and delete, edit, and schedule all posts. The admin user that the WordPress installation creates has an Administrator user role, as should the first user account you create for yourself. If you're going to have other people blogging with you, chances are that they should have one of the other, less powerful roles.

Editor

The Editor role is one step below the Administrator role. Although a user with Administrator privileges has access to both sides of the blog—the technical side (such as themes, plug-ins, and users) and the content side (pages, posts, and comments)—a user with Editor privileges has full control of content only. An Editor can create posts, comments, links, and pages, as well as edit anything that another user creates. This person can even edit content that is created by an Administrator.

In a multiauthor blogging environment, give this role to someone who's in charge of all aspects of content, sort of like an editor-in-chief of a newspaper. This person can decide what gets published when.

Author

The Author role is even more focused on blog content than the Editor role is. An Author can write and publish posts, as well as edit any comments on those posts. This person can't edit or approve comments on other people's work, however.

This role is suited for someone who (to continue the newspaper analogy) can serve as a staff writer. You trust this user to write well and to publish only things that are worthy of your blog.

Contributor

I like to think of the people in Contributor roles as freelancers working on assignment. They can write posts and create pages, but they can't publish anything themselves. Everything that a Contributor user writes is submitted for review. The post is marked as pending review until a user in an Editor or Administrator role approves and publishes it. Contributors can't approve comments on their own posts or edit their own posts.

Assign this role to people whom you're trying out on your blog. As you gain confidence in their abilities, you can promote them to the Author role.

Subscriber

As the name suggests, a person in the Subscriber role isn't able to create posts, edit users, or do any sort of administration of the blog. You can set your blog so that only registered Subscribers can post comments; I explain how in the next section, "Registering users." You also can allow people to register themselves as users, generally in the Subscriber role; again, see the next section for details.

Subscribers can log in to the WordPress admin area, but they can change only their user information (set a new password or change a bio).

Registering users

You don't have to add every user to your blog manually. This process could get quite cumbersome if you require people to register with your site before they can leave comments. (If you get more than a few readers, you won't want to have to create their user accounts by hand.) Luckily, WordPress provides a way for people to register themselves. This feature is turned off by default, but you can enable it very simply.

In the Add New User section of the Users screen, you see a line that says *Users cannot currently register themselves, but you can manually create users here*. Clicking the words *register themselves* takes you to the General Settings page of your blog (which I cover fully in Chapter 5). **Figure 3.11** shows the membership options.

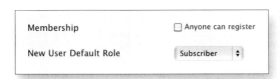

Figure 3.11
Membership options.

The Membership section has one option that's disabled by default: Anyone Can Register. Check this box to allow any visitor to your site to register as a user.

You can also set the role for any user account registered in this fashion by making a choice from the New User Default Role drop-down menu (**Figure 3.12**). The default setting is Subscriber.

Figure 3.12
Assigning a role to a new user.

tip   I suggest that you keep this menu set to Subscriber. You don't want random people to create their own posts on your blog, and you certainly don't want just anyone to administer your blog.

Changing user roles

During the course of your blog's life, you may want to promote someone from a Contributor to an Editor, or make an Author into a Contributor just for fun. (Isn't holding power over something a joy?) All you have to do is follow these steps:

1. Click the Users link in the Dashboard to open the Users screen.

2. In the list of your blog's users, check the box next to the user whose role you want to change.

3. From the Change Role To drop-down menu above the list of users (**Figure 3.13**), choose the new role you want to assign.

Figure 3.13 Pick a new role from the menu.

4. Click the Change button.

   That's it. Now the user now has more (or less) power.

 note   **Only Administrator users can change user roles.**

Deleting users

 note   **Keep in mind that there's no way to reverse a deletion, so delete only when you're certain that you no longer want that user around.**

Deleting a user is much like changing a user's role. Follow these steps:

1. Click the Users link in the Dashboard to open the Users screen.

2. Hover your mouse over the user you want to delete.

   You'll see two links appear: Edit and Delete (**Figure 3.14**).

Figure 3.14 These two links appear whenever you hover over a user.

3. Click the Delete link.

The Delete Users screen opens (**Figure 3.15**). Because WordPress assumes that all that users are making content for your blog, you have to tell it what you want it to do with this user's content (if any).

Figure 3.15 The Delete Users screen.

4. Choose an option to specify what to do with the user's content.

   You have two choices:

   • **Delete All Posts and Links.** When you select this radio button, the user you're deleting never existed as far as WordPress is concerned. All of her posts and links will be deleted from your site.

   • **Attribute All Posts and Links to x.** In this case, x is another user. This option is the more interesting, and more clever, of the two choices. The user account will still be deleted, which means that the user won't be able to log in and add more content, but the existing content won't be deleted. Instead, the deleted user's posts and links will be displayed under the user name of the person you choose from this drop-down menu.

   note Even if you delete all of a user's posts, comments on those posts will remain on display. If you want to get rid of all traces of that user on your blog, you'll have to delete the comments on his posts manually. Keep in mind, though, that deleting comments generally is considered to be bad form unless the comments are abusive in some way. Use your power wisely.

5. Click the Confirm Deletion button to delete the user forever.

4

The Dashboard

The Dashboard (**Figure 4.1** on the next page) is the first thing you see when you log in to any installation of WordPress. It's your captain's chair, the tower from which you overlook the grandeur of your digital kingdom, the window into your blog, and a dozen more clichés.

The Dashboard provides information at a glance about a variety of WordPress-related items through eight modules:

- Right Now
- Recent Comments
- Incoming Links
- Plugins
- QuickPress
- Recent Drafts
- WordPress Blog
- Other WordPress News

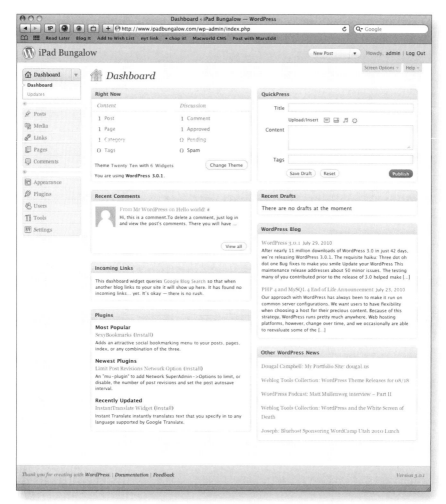

Figure 4.1 The WordPress Dashboard, in all its glory.

Out of the box, the Dashboard's customization options are limited, but they can be expanded with—you guessed it—plug-ins. This isn't to say that you don't have any options out of the gate, though. As long as you're logged in as a user in the Administrator role, you can change a few things.

In this chapter, I take a look at the anatomy of the Dashboard. Along the way, I point out what you can change.

Right Here: Right Now

At the top of the Dashboard, you see the Right Now module (**Figure 4.2**).

Figure 4.2 Right Now displays an easy-to-read overview of your blog's content and gives you a quick way to change your blog's theme.

As you can see, the Right Now module displays some statistics about your blog in two columns: Content and Discussion. Each entry, no matter which column it appears in, is a hyperlink. A fresh installation of WordPress comes with one post and a comment to give you a good starting place. Clicking one of the statistics links takes you to the related section of WordPress, as follows:

- The Posts link takes you to the Posts module, where you can edit or create posts (depending on your role).

- The Pages link takes you to the Pages module.

- The Categories link shows you how many categories you currently have in your blog. Click this link to add, edit, or delete categories.

- The Tags link shows you how many tags you currently have in your blog. Click this link to add, edit, or delete tags.

- The Discussion column has four categories: Comments (total comments), Approved (number of approved comments), Pending (number of pending comments), and Spam (number of spam comments). When the number in any of those categories is greater than zero, you can click the link to perform comment-specific actions.

Below all that information about the content of your blog, you get some info about the blog itself: the current theme, which determines what your blog looks like, and the number of widgets the theme is using. (See Chapter 12 for details on themes and widgets.) Clicking the Widgets link takes you to the Widgets module, which allows you to add or remove widgets. You can change your current theme by clicking the Change Theme button.

Finally, the Right Now module displays the version of WordPress you're running. If a new version is available, two things happen: A note alerts you to update your software (**Figure 4.3**), and a new button appears in the Right Now module, labeled *Update to 3.0.1* (or whatever the current version is).

WordPress 3.0.1 is available! Please update now.   Screen Option

🏠 *Dashboard*

Figure 4.3 When a WordPress update is available, an alert pops up on the Dashboard.

Meeting the Public: Comments and Links

The two modules right below Right Now concern the lifeblood of any blog: comments and external links. You'll never forget the first time someone comments on one of your blog posts, and you'll be thrilled when you find the first Web site *not* run by you that's linking to your blog.

Recent Comments module

As you might expect, the Recent Comments module (**Figure 4.4**) displays recent comments that folks have left on your blog. It also alerts you to any comments that are awaiting moderation. A pending comment is highlighted in yellow, and the pound sign (#) is a link directly to that comment. You can also click the View All button in the bottom-right corner to manage all the comments on your blog.

Figure 4.4 Recent Comments are displayed in this module.

Incoming Links module

The Incoming Links module (**Figure 4.5**) is a great way to see what other people are saying about your blog on their blogs. This feature uses Google Blog Search to see what blogs are linking to yours and reports back to you. When you first install WordPress, there won't be any links to your blog, so your module will look like Figure 4.5. As you start to blog, though, you'll start to build your audience, and people will start linking to you. It won't happen overnight, but with some work, it'll happen sooner than you think.

Incoming Links

This dashboard widget queries Google Blog Search so that when another blog links to your site it will show up here. It has found no incoming links... yet. It's okay — there is no rush.

Figure 4.5 Incoming Links tells you how many people are (or aren't) linking to your blog.

You can customize this module to a degree by hovering over the module's title, which causes a Configure link to appear in the right end of the header. Clicking the Configure link expands the module, as you see in **Figure 4.6**.

Incoming Links   Cancel

Enter the RSS feed URL here:

http://blogsearch.google.com/blogsearch_feeds?scoring=

How many items would you like to display?   10

☐ Display item date?

(Submit)

Figure 4.6 You can plug in the RSS feed of your favorite blog search engine here and make the Incoming Links module display what you want to see.

You can set the following options in the expanded Incoming Links module:

- **RSS feed.** By default, this module uses Google Blog Search, but if you prefer to use another search engine that provides an RSS feed of results, you can enter the URL of its RSS feed here. (I discuss RSS feeds in more detail in Chapter 5.)

- **Number of items to display.** Choose the number you want from the drop-down menu. You can display 1 to 20 items.

- **Display date.** If you check this box, the date of the link appears alongside the link itself.

Whatever you do in this expanded module, click Submit when you're done to tell WordPress to accept your changes.

 note   You can't customize this module too much, and the same goes for the rest of the modules featured in this chapter.

Plugins

The next module in the Dashboard is Plugins, which displays plug-ins in three categories: Most Popular, Newest Plugins, and Recently Updated (**Figure 4.7**). Clicking a plug-in's name takes you to its page in the WordPress Plugins directory. You can also install one of the listed plug-ins just by clicking the Install link next to it. I explore plug-ins in depth in Chapter 14.

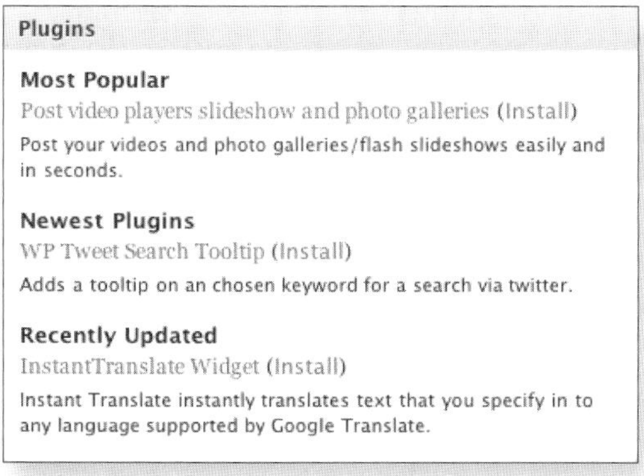

Plugins

Most Popular
Post video players slideshow and photo galleries (Install)
Post your videos and photo galleries/flash slideshows easily and in seconds.

Newest Plugins
WP Tweet Search Tooltip (Install)
Adds a tooltip on an chosen keyword for a search via twitter.

Recently Updated
InstantTranslate Widget (Install)
Instant Translate instantly translates text that you specify in to any language supported by Google Translate.

Figure 4.7 This module high-lights plug-ins that may be of interest to you.

QuickPress

QuickPress is a great way to get an idea from your mind onto your blog in no time flat (**Figure 4.8**). As the name implies, this module is all about making it very easy to post to your blog. I cover posting from top to bottom in Chapter 6, but now I'll talk about the trade-offs you make for the speed of QuickPress.

The QuickPress module allows you to write blog posts that include text, video, audio, and images, but you have to use HTML to format the post.

Furthermore, you can't assign categories (though you can enter tags), and the myriad formatting options available in the far more robust Add New Post section just plain aren't available.

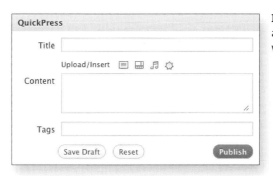

Figure 4.8 QuickPress offers a fast way to write a blog post, with some limitations.

Why would you ever use QuickPress, given these limitations? Well, notice that Save Draft button at the bottom of the module? I don't know about you, but I often have a brilliant idea for a post, and if I wait too long to write it down, the idea just vanishes. QuickPress is a great way to jot down blog-post ideas and save them as drafts.

I cover the differences between a draft and a post in Chapter 6 and provide more details on drafts in the next section of this chapter.

Recent Drafts

A *draft* is a blog post, or page, that isn't ready for public consumption. Think of a draft as being a work in progress. Visitors to your blog don't see drafts; only people who are logged in to your blog's Dashboard can see your drafts, and only if they have the proper permissions.

The Dashboard's Recent Drafts module (**Figure 4.9**) displays any drafts that you've saved. Each draft shows up as a link, and when you click that link, you go directly to the edit screen for that draft. Clicking the View All button lists all the drafts that you currently have saved.

Figure 4.9 Recent Drafts lists all the drafts you can see on your blog.

WordPress Blog

The WordPress Blog module displays, by default, the two most recent entries from the official WordPress blog. You can see the entry's title, a brief excerpt, and the date on which it was published. Clicking the title of the post takes you to that post's page on the WordPress blog.

Hovering over the title of the module reveals a Configure link. When you click that link, you see all the options for the module (**Figure 4.10**).

Figure 4.10 The WordPress Blog module, expanded.

Here's what the options mean:

- **RSS-feed URL.** Enter the URL of the feed you want this module to display. As you can see in Figure 4.10, the WordPress news blog is the default, but you can enter any valid RSS URL. An RSS URL, for those who are unfamiliar with the concept, is also called a blog's *feed*. It's a file that lists all the recent updates on your blog, and allows people to subscribe to your blog and read your updates in an application called a *news reader*. (Google Reader and NetNewsWire are two examples of such applications.)

- **Feed title.** The default is WordPress Blog, but you can change the title to anything you want; then the module's name changes in the interface. You could use this setting in combination with the RSS-feed setting to display a different blog's content in this module and have it labeled as such. Neato.

- **Display of item content.** Because this module is a mini-RSS reader, it only makes sense that you can display the content of entries. Only excerpts are shown in this module's limited space; disable this option if you want to see just titles.

- **Display of item author.** In keeping with the mini-RSS reader idea, you can also display the author of the entry if it's available in the feed.

- **Display of item date.** This option displays the date when an item from this RSS feed was posted.

Keeping Current: Other WordPress News

The final module of the Dashboard, Other WordPress News (**Figure 4.11**), showcases blogs that are either written by WordPress developers or devoted to WordPress.

Other WordPress News
Weblog Tools Collection: Drive Traffic to Old Content with "Tweet Old Post" Plugin
Dougal Campbell: My Portfolio Site: dougal.us
Weblog Tools Collection: WordPress Theme Releases for 08/18
WordPress Podcast: Matt Mullenweg interview – Part II
Weblog Tools Collection: WordPress and the White Screen of Death

Figure 4.11 The Other WordPress News module.

 note This module is also known as the Secondary Feed module.

When you mouse over the module and click the Configure link that appears, you see the same options that are available in the WordPress Blog module, and they all function the same way (**Figure 4.12**).

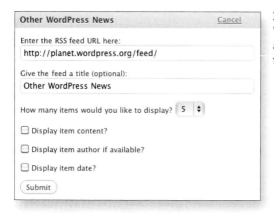

Figure 4.12 The Other WordPress News module allows you to display any RSS feed you want.

Customizing the Dashboard

You're an individual (and so am I; we have so much in common!), and I'm sure that you'd like to make the Dashboard all yours. WordPress gives you the option to customize the appearance of your Dashboard. In the top-right corner, you see a gray rectangle labeled Screen Options (refer to Figure 4.1 earlier in this chapter). When you click it, a menu of display options for your Dashboard appears (**Figure 4.13**).

Figure 4.13 The Dashboard screen options. Anything with a check is displayed; unchecked items are not.

All the modules available for your Dashboard are listed here. By default, they're all checked, which means that they appear in your Dashboard. If you clear a module's check box, that module is removed from your Dashboard. (To bring it back, just check its box again at any time.)

The Screen Options menu also lets you customize the number of columns in your Dashboard, from one to four.

In addition, you can rearrange the modules in your Dashboard by dragging and dropping them. When you hover over the header of a module, the cursor turns into a cross; click and hold the mouse button to move the module around on the page. When you release the mouse button, the module snaps into place.

Beyond the Dashboard

The top of the Dashboard—and every WordPress administrative page, for that matter—features the controls shown in **Figure 4.14**.

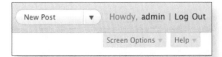

Figure 4.14 The New Post button sits at the top of every page in the WordPress admin interface.

The New Post button takes you to the Posts page. If you click the arrow next to it, a menu drops down, listing shortcuts to other sections of the WordPress admin interface (**Figure 4.15**). You can jump directly to Drafts, New Page, Upload, and Comments, each of which I cover in full in later chapters.

Figure 4.15 These shortcuts are listed when you click the triangle next to the New Post link at the top of a WordPress page.

The controls at the far right end (refer to Figure 4.14) contains a mix of links to internal and external resources:

- **User name.** The first link is your user name, which takes you to your profile page (see Chapter 3).

- **Log Out.** The Log Out link logs you out of the WordPress administrative interface.

- **Help.** Clicking this link reveals a help page for the Dashboard. This link is contextual, so when you go to different pages in the WordPress admin interface, the Help link relates to the page that you're viewing.

tip The Dashboard also includes a link to the WordPress Forums page (http://wordpress.org/support), which provides lots of support information.

5

Futureproofing Your Blog

There's one last bit of business to take care of before I delve into populating your blog with some awesome content: your blog's settings. This chapter is titled "Futureproofing Your Blog" because the decisions you make now will affect how you and your readers interact with your blog.

Clicking the Settings link in the left navigation bar, which appears on all pages in the WordPress administrative interface (**Figure 5.1** on the next page), takes you, surprisingly enough, to your blog's Settings page. (You start in the General Settings section.) In addition to setting general options, you specify on this page how you write posts, how those posts are displayed, and who can read what.

Figure 5.1 The WordPress navigation bar. All your settings dreams await you.

General Settings

When you first click the Settings link, you see the general settings for your blog. Many of these settings are defined in the wp-config.php file (refer to Chapter 2), but you can change them here at any time (**Figure 5.2**).

Figure 5.2 Your blog's General Settings page.

note After you change any of the settings listed in this chapter, make sure to click the Save Changes button at the bottom of the page. If you don't, your changes won't be saved, and you'll need to make them again.

Blog name and tag line

The Site Title and Tagline options (**Figure 5.3**) are often used in a blog's header, so make sure that you like the name you give your blog.

| Site Title | iPad Bungalow | |
| Tagline | Just another WordPress site
site is about. | *In a few words, explain what this* |

Figure 5.3 Your site's title and tag line are often the things that people remember best.

 note Something to keep in mind: Should your blog succeed, there's a chance that you'll be known by your blog's name. In some circles, I'm known as Blankbaby, which a weaker man might not be able to handle. Name your blog well.

WordPress and blog URLs

The WordPress Address (URL) and Site Address (URL) options (**Figure 5.4**) aren't the same, though it certainly seems that they would be. The WordPress URL points to the directory on the Web server that houses your installation of WordPress, whereas the site URL is the address people enter to get to your blog. In most cases, these URLs are the same, but you can separate the files that make up the WordPress application itself from the contents of your blog, as I discuss later in this chapter.

| WordPress address (URL) | http://www.ipadbungalow.com | |
| Site address (URL) | http://www.ipadbungalow.com
want your site homepage to be different from the directory you installed WordPress. | *Enter the address here if you* |

Figure 5.4 WordPress Address points to where WordPress itself is installed; Site Address is the URL of your blog.

Storing WordPress and content files together

WordPress, as you know, is made up of various folders and files. By default, those files are stored in the same directory, as you see in **Figure 5.5**. But if your blog is just one component of a multifaceted Web site, you may want to have tighter control of your directory structure.

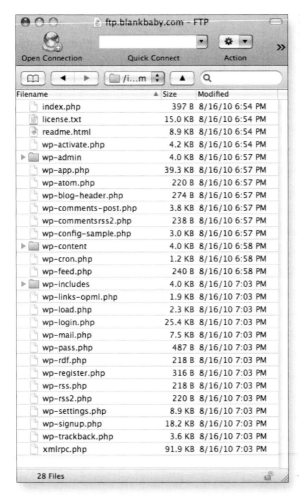

Figure 5.5 A directory that contains both WordPress and blog files.

Confused? Consider a concrete example: the WordPress for All blog. I uploaded the contents of the wordpress folder, which I got from WordPress. org, to my Web site's root directory. As you see in Figure 5.5, that folder is now chockablock with all the files and directories that WordPress needs.

Separating WordPress and content files

Moving all those WordPress files into their own directory would really neaten things. This change won't have any noticeable ramifications for your readers but will affect the people who create content for your blog, no matter what roles they play. (Flip back to Chapter 3 for details on user roles.)

Again, consider the example WordPress for All blog. As it's set up at the moment, people log into the administrative side by going to www.*yourblogname*.com/wp-admin. Moving the WordPress files to their own directory would change the URL for logging in to the admin interface.

Separating WordPress and content files is easy. Just follow these steps:

1. Create a new directory to hold the WordPress files.

    For this exercise, create a directory called wordpress.

    Next, because you're moving the entire WordPress application, you need to make sure that WordPress knows where all its files are before you move them.

2. On the General Settings page, change the WordPress Address (URL) option to reflect the future home of your WordPress installation.

3. Click Save Changes.

    You'll get an error message. Don't worry about it.

4. Move all your WordPress files to your new wordpress directory, but leave the index.php file in the root directory (**Figure 5.6**).

Figure 5.6 WordPress installed in the wordpress directory. Much neater.

note **The index.php file makes the blog URL work.**

The index.php file needs one edit; then you'll be all done.

5. Open the index.php file in your favorite text editor, and look for the following section:

```
require('./wp-blog-header.php');
```

This bit of code tells the index file where your WordPress files live, and because you just moved them, the code is pointing to the wrong place. (By default, this file assumes that all the WordPress files are in the directory where it resides.)

6. Add the name of the new directory to the code in Step 5, using this format:

```
require('./directory/wp-blog-header.php');
```

For this exercise, you moved the files to a directory called wordpress, so change the code to this:

```
require('./wordpress/wp-blog-header.php');
```

7. Save the file.

Everything works exactly as it did before, but your blog is a little better organized, as a glance at the General Settings page shows (**Figure 5.7**).

Figure 5.7 New URL settings.

Email address

The E-Mail Address setting (**Figure 5.8**) requires a valid email address. WordPress will send notifications about your blog in general to the address you enter, and you'll want to get them (as you see in "Notification options" later in this chapter).

Figure 5.8 All email notifications will be sent to the address you enter here.

Membership options

I cover these options in Chapter 3, so I'll keep this discussion brief.

In the Membership section (**Figure 5.9**), checking the Anyone Can Register check box allows visitors to your blog to create user accounts. (By default, this option is turned off, so no one can register.) You can also set what role is automatically assigned to new users, with the default being the least powerful role: Subscriber.

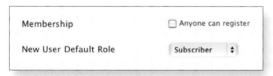

Figure 5.9 Do you want people to register their own accounts on your blog? Make sure that you give them a proper default role.

Time options

Time is our most precious resource, and it isn't renewable. Luckily, WordPress gives you a lot of control of how time is displayed and kept in your WordPress blog. You can set the time zone, date and time formats, and the day on which your week starts.

Time zone

Setting your time zone (**Figure 5.10**) is straightforward, and support for daylight saving time (DST) is built in. From the extensive Timezone drop-down menu, just choose the time zone your blog should follow.

Timezone	UTC+0	⬍	UTC time is 2010-08-21 20:00:15
	Choose a city in the same timezone as you.		

Figure 5.10 The WordPress Timezone setting automatically accounts for daylight saving time.

note   WordPress employs Coordinated Universal Time (UTC), which is known casually as Greenwich Mean Time. Technically, UTC and GMT have some slight differences, but for purposes of this discussion, they're the same.

Date and time formats

The Date Format and Time Format settings (**Figure 5.11**) are a little more interesting. WordPress time-stamps all the content in your blog for a variety of reasons, and this section allows you to specify how the time is displayed. As you can see in Figure 5.11, the most common date and time formats are listed. Just select the one that suits you, or select a custom format.

Date Format	⦿ August 21, 2010
	◯ 2010/08/21
	◯ 08/21/2010
	◯ 21/08/2010
	◯ Custom: F j, Y August 21, 2010
	Documentation on date formatting. Click "Save Changes" to update sample output.
Time Format	⦿ 8:00 pm
	◯ 8:00 PM
	◯ 20:00
	◯ Custom: g:i a 8:00 pm

Figure 5.11 You have several options for displaying the date in your blog.

The time function of WordPress is written in PHP, as is the rest of WordPress, which means that your customization options are pretty wide open.

 tip **If you want more information about the various date parameters that WordPress accepts, check out the PHP date-function documentation at http://us3.php.net/date.**

 note **You need to save your changes before you see a preview of the new time format.**

Table 5.1 lists some of the most common date formats.

Table 5.1 Date Formats

Code	Resulting Date
F j, Y	August 23, 2011
F-m-d	2011-08-23
d.m.F	23.08.2011
g:i a	7:03 pm
g:i a e	7:03 p.m. UTC
g:i a T	8:10 p.m. GMT
H:i:s	20:12:07

Start of week

Finally, this section of the General Settings page allows to you tell WordPress which day of the week to treat as the start of the week. The default setting is Monday, but you can choose any day of the week from the Week Starts On drop down-menu.

Writing Settings

The settings I discuss in this section define how you post on your blog. From enabling the ability to post via email to determining the size of the box in which you type your posts, the Writing Settings page is the place to set your writing options.

Accessing the Writing Settings page is easy. Just click the Writing link in the Settings section.

Posting from WordPress

The posting settings, shown in **Figure 5.12**, affect the experience of posting on your blog from within the WordPress application itself.

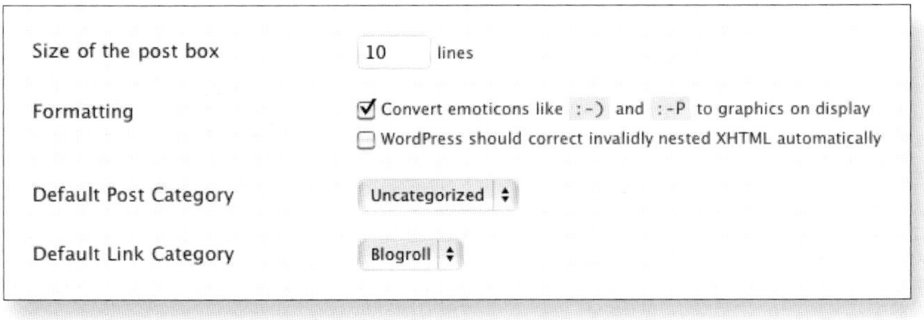

Size of the post box	10	lines
Formatting	☑ Convert emoticons like `:-)` and `:-P` to graphics on display	
	☐ WordPress should correct invalidly nested XHTML automatically	
Default Post Category	Uncategorized ⬍	
Default Link Category	Blogroll ⬍	

Figure 5.12 Posting options abound in the Writing Settings page.

Post-box size

By default, the post box is 10 lines long, which I find to be more than big enough for my purposes. If you need more space to write, feel free to change the Size of the Post Box value. The maximum is 100 lines, though I can't imagine why you would want your post box to be that large.

Formatting: Emoticons

Emoticons (also known as *smileys*) are all the rage with the kids these days, or so I'm told, and WordPress can cater to the emoticon set. If you check the pertinent check box in the Formatting section, WordPress automatically converts emoticons to graphic representations of the various smiley faces (**Figure 5.13**).

Figure 5.13 Emoticons make me smile.

Enabling emoticons allows both commenters and bloggers to use them.

tip **You can also trigger this functionality automatically by typing certain key terms, such as :lol: and :cool:.**

note **For a full list of the default emoticons and the text needed to insert them, check out the official Smilies WordPress Codex page at http://codex.wordpress.org/Using_Smilies. ;)**

You can add your own custom smilies by replacing the files in *root*/wp-includes/images/smilies, where *root* is the directory in which WordPress is installed. Be sure to replace the files with small GIF files that are named the same way.

Formatting: XHTML

The second check box in the Formatting section—WordPress Should Correct Invalidly Nested XHTML Automatically—is decidedly less whimsical. XHTML is a stricter form of HTML, with which you are no doubt familiar. Both XHTML and HTML are tag-based languages. XHTML, however, requires every tag to have a closing tag, whereas HTML is a little more lax in that department. If you want your blog's code to validate, you should check this check box; otherwise, you can safely ignore it. (That sound you just heard was Web geeks everywhere passing out after reading this advice.)

Default post and link categories

You can set default categories for both posts and links. Choose a category from the Default Post Category or Default Link Category drop-down menu, and any new post or link automatically falls into that category. (You can add more categories or remove the defaults on individual posts and links when you edit them. See Chapter 6 for information about settings for posts and Chapter 10 for details on links.).

Links and posts don't share category lists, so you'll see a different set of values in each drop-down menu. (By default, the only post category you see is Uncategorized, and the only link category is Blogroll.) It would be nice if you could have WordPress *not* apply a category to new posts and links. I don't know about you, but I blog about a wide range of topics, and no single category applies to all my posts and links. Perhaps a future version of WordPress will allow me—and bloggers like me—to turn off default categorization.

Posting with Press This

The Press This link (**Figure 5.14**)—short for *WordPress this*—is actually a JavaScript bookmarklet. *Bookmarklets* are simple additions to your browser that don't actually bookmark Web sites; instead, they perform a task (or series of tasks) based on what Web site you're viewing. Drag the Press This bookmarklet into your browser's bookmarks bar, and you can post to your blog simply by clicking the link.

Figure 5.14 The Press This bookmarklet installed in Safari.

The Press This bookmarklet does a clever thing: It inserts the title and link of the page you're viewing into a post. Then you can simply post the link or add some commentary.

Press This also makes it very easy to post links, text, and video that you find while surfing the Net.

note   **Remember to properly attribute anything that you use from another source (typically by linking back to the source).**

When you click Press This while viewing a Web page, different things can happen, depending on what type of Web site you're on. If you click the bookmarklet while you're viewing a YouTube video, for example, a post window opens, displaying the embed code for that video. In Chapter 7, I cover all the different ways you can use Press This.

Posting via email

Wouldn't it be great if you could email your blog and have it post the contents of that email? WordPress gives you that capability, though this feature is pretty rudimentary at this point. You have to provide WordPress login credentials for a POP email account. The account must be accessible via POP, because WordPress actually logs in to this account and checks for messages.

The idea is pretty simple: You set up a secret email address that WordPress can check (the General Settings page provides three suggestions; **Figure 5.15**), provide login information to WordPress, and then send an email to the secret address. WordPress checks the email account and posts the contents of the email to your blog, using the subject as the title of the post and the body of the message as the body of the post.

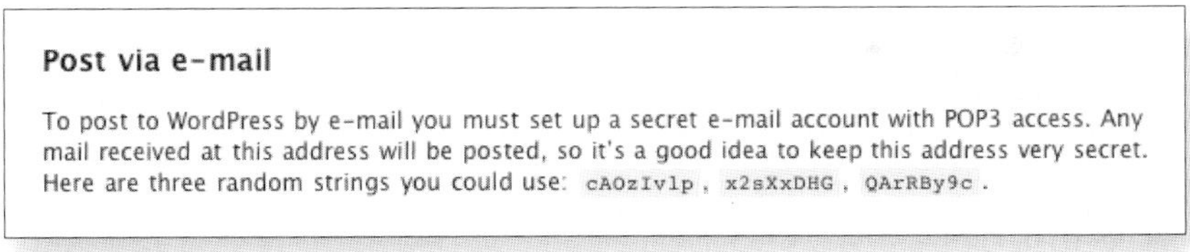

Post via e-mail

To post to WordPress by e-mail you must set up a secret e-mail account with POP3 access. Any mail received at this address will be posted, so it's a good idea to keep this address very secret. Here are three random strings you could use: cAOzIv1p , x2sXxDHG , QArRBy9c .

Figure 5.15 WordPress suggests three secret addresses.

Sadly, WordPress can't check this account for email on its own. You have to visit a URL that fires off a process that checks the account and posts the emailed post. (That URL is www.*yourblogname*.com/*wordpress*/wp-mail.php, where *wordpress* is the directory where you've installed WordPress.) The situation isn't ideal, but you can use a couple of work-arounds:

- To the footer of your blog, add a frame including some code that visits the address where the wp-mail.php file is located. Every time one of your blog pages is loaded, WordPress checks the email account for emailed posts.

- Use **cron**, a Unix program that runs tasks on a schedule, to visit
  wp-mail.php at regular intervals. Check your Web host's documentation
  to see whether you have access to **cron** on its servers.

 note   I should point out that posting via email doesn't support posting
attachments, which means that you can't email a picture to your
WordPress blog and have it post automatically. You can add this
functionality with a plug-in, however. I discuss plug-ins in
Chapter 14.

You need to provide WordPress the following information before you can
post via email (**Figure 5.16**):

Mail Server	mail.example.com	Port	110
Login Name	login@example.com		
Password	password		
Default Mail Category	Uncategorized ⬍		

Figure 5.16 Settings for the Post via E-Mail feature.

- **Mail Server.** This section actually has two parts: the Mail Server text
  box and the Port text box. As you see in Figure 5.16, you need to provide
  the address of your mail server so that WordPress knows where to
  check for the emailed posts. The port number is set to the default for
  POP3 (110), which is the only kind of email account WordPress can check.
  If your email server uses a different port, make sure to set it here. (Ask
  your postmaster for this information if you don't have it.)

- **Login Name.** In this text box, enter the name of the account that
  WordPress will use to log in to the account. Typically, this account is the
  same as the email address used for the email posting.

- **Password.** This setting is the password of the email account you set up
  for mobile blogging.

 note   WordPress doesn't obscure what you type in this text box, so don't
enter a password where prying eyes may be lurking.

- **Default Mail Category.** Much as you set a default category for every post and link in WordPress, you can set a default category for posts sent via email. You may think that having a default category for regular posts and links is silly, but this option makes perfect sense. Adding a category like Posts from On the Go or Moblogging tells your readers that you tapped the post out on a tiny keyboard, so it may contain a few more typos than usual.

 Although I think this WordPress feature isn't ready for prime time, it's worth noting that blogs hosted on WordPress.com don't get this functionality at all.

Publishing remotely

You have two choices for posting on your blog:

- Use the posting tools in the WordPress administration interface.

- Use a third-party desktop/mobile application to post to your blog.

The second option is known as *remote publishing* in WordPress speak.

The protocols required to use a third-party blogging application (see the nearby sidebar) are disabled by default in WordPress. Because most people use WordPress to post, the developers decided to close off all unnecessary protocols and possible attack vectors.

That being said, I'm unaware of any security holes in remote-posting protocols, so one of the first things I do in a WordPress installation is enable both Atom Publishing Protocol and XML-RPC in the Remote Publishing section (**Figure 5.17**). If you don't plan to use a third-party blogging tool, you should leave these protocols disabled.

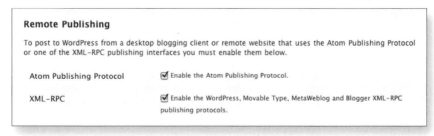

Remote Publishing

To post to WordPress from a desktop blogging client or remote website that uses the Atom Publishing Protocol or one of the XML-RPC publishing interfaces you must enable them below.

Atom Publishing Protocol   ☑ Enable the Atom Publishing Protocol.

XML-RPC   ☑ Enable the WordPress, Movable Type, MetaWeblog and Blogger XML-RPC publishing protocols.

Figure 5.17 Enabling remote-posting protocols in WordPress.

Why Even Use a Desktop Blogging Client?

These clients offer several advantages over the WordPress posting form:

- Because they're full-fledged applications, they have access to features of your operating system (spell checking being a big one, for me at least).

- You can write drafts and store them locally, in case you want to mull over your subject for a while.

- You can use one application to post to multiple blogs.

Here are a few blogging clients to check out.

Windows

- **BlogJet.** Lots of Windows bloggers swear by this tool. It's a little pricey at $39.95, but it has a well-thought-out interface and a slew of features that let you publish one post to multiple blogs at the same time, create drafts, and automatically insert the title of whatever you're listening to in iTunes or Windows Media Player. Get it at www.codingrobots.com/blogjet.

- **Windows Live Writer.** Live Writer is a free blog editor from Microsoft. If you're familiar with Microsoft Office, this app will feel like home to you. Get it at http://get.live.com/writer/overview.

Mac OS X

- **ecto.** This blogging client offers a ton of features. You can create Amazon.com affiliate links, search a wide range of media, and perform many more tasks within the app itself. ecto costs $19.95 and is available at http://infinite-sushi.com/software/ecto.

- **MarsEdit.** My blogger editor of choice, MarsEdit doesn't have as many bells and whistles as ecto, but I like its streamlined interface better. MarsEdit costs $39.95 at www.red-sweater.com/marsedit.

This list isn't meant to be exhaustive. Think of it as being a jumping-off point for exploring blogging tools for your platform of choice.

Using update services

You started a blog because you want people to read what you post, right? One way to get readers in the crowded blogosphere is to ping an update service—a central place that keeps a list of recently updated blogs. When you post a new entry to your blog, you ping (tell) the update service that you posted something, and the service duly notes it. When someone asks that service for recently updated posts, it returns a link to your new post, along with other recently posted entries.

You can find lots of update services out there, which has led Automattic (the company that runs WordPress.com, made up of many of the people behind WordPress itself) to create Ping-o-Matic. Ping-o-Matic is a central update service that updates the other update services (whoa—meta!). WordPress ships configured to tell Ping-o-Matic whenever you post something, and then the service informs a host of other update services.

You can remove Ping-o-Matic simply by deleting that entry in the Update Services section (**Figure 5.18**), or you can add another update service by pasting the proper URL into the text box. (The update service you're adding should have documentation that includes the proper URL to enter.) Be sure to separate URLs with line breaks by pressing Enter or Return after each URL.

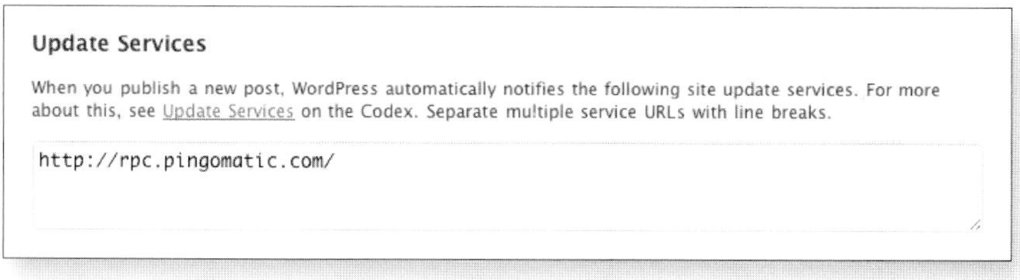

Update Services

When you publish a new post, WordPress automatically notifies the following site update services. For more about this, see Update Services on the Codex. Separate multiple service URLs with line breaks.

http://rpc.pingomatic.com/

Figure 5.18 The update service you list here tells people when your blog has been updated.

Reading Settings

The other side of the blogging coin is reading. Your blog won't be much fun if no one reads it, though don't be fooled into thinking that your blog isn't a success if you reach a small number of people. A small blog that you use to keep in touch with friends and relatives is just as important as a large political or tech blog with millions of readers. (Personally, I find small personal blogs to be much more interesting than large professional blogs, and I've written for some of those large blogs!)

You do have a few decisions to make about how your blog content is consumed, no matter how many readers you end up with. The Reading Settings (listed below the Settings section) is where those decisions happen.

Setting the front page

Some people refer to WordPress as being a content management system (CMS), and with the addition of the Front Page Displays setting (**Figure 5.19**), this characterization is truer now than it's ever been.

Figure 5.19
WordPress isn't limited to displaying a list of posts on your home page. You can set it to display a static page instead.

The traditional WordPress installation simply displays a list of the most recent posts on the index page (the first page people see when they navigate to your blog), and that's still the default setting.

Selecting a static page as your front page, however, opens some interesting possibilities. You can create a page that provides static information about you or your product (as I discuss in Chapter 8), which makes your blog look more like a traditional Web site.

You can also designate a page as a Posts page, which lists your blog posts separately. So when people visit your blog's index page, they see a page full of whatever information you want to give them, with a link to another page that is, for all intents and purposes, your blog. This option makes it a breeze to create a dynamic site with content that's easy to update.

If you decide to set up your blog in this manner, but you don't see any pages listed in the Front Page and Posts Page drop-down menus, there's a simple explanation: You have to create the pages before you complete these settings.

No matter where you decide to list your posts, whether it be on the index page or on a subpage, you have the option of showing as many or as few posts as you want. Just type the number in the Blog Pages Show at Most x Posts text box (refer to Figure 5.19). Some blogs (such as video and photo blogs) are well suited to showing a single post on a page at a time; others (such as links blogs) benefit from more posts per page.

 The more posts you have on a page, the longer that page will take to load, which may be a consideration if you have many readers who come to your site without a broadband connection.

Configuring your feeds

Blogs wouldn't be as popular as they are without syndication feeds. These feeds are actually text files formatted in such a way as to be easily parsed by clients called *feed readers* or *RSS readers*. If you think of your blog as a magazine, your feed is a way for readers to subscribe to your publication. Just as the editor of a magazine has to decide what to publish, you have to decide what information to include in your feeds. Remember that feeds are important to a blog; a good feed is one that makes people want to keep reading.

Number of posts

The first decision you have to make is how many posts to include in the feed. This setting is important when a person first subscribes to your feed, because it determines how many posts he gets right off the bat. The default setting, 10 (**Figure 5.20**), is a good number in my opinion—just enough to get someone up to speed on your posts and not enough to overwhelm him.

Syndication feeds show the most recent	10	items
For each article in a feed, show	⦿ Full text ◯ Summary	
Encoding for pages and feeds	UTF-8	*The character encoding of your site (UTF-8 is recommended. if you are adventurous there are some other encodings)*

Figure 5.20 Options for your blog's feed.

Feed content

The second decision is much more basic: How much content do you want to provide in your feed? You have to keep in mind that people who subscribe to your blog's feed are reading it in their feed readers, not by loading your Web site. As a result, they won't see any ads that you may have on your site, which makes some site owners nervous. You can give subscribers just a taste of your post and force them to visit your site to read the whole thing by selecting the Summary radio button (refer to Figure 5.20).

I think this method is foolish, however, for a couple of reasons:

- If someone has gone to the trouble of subscribing to your blog, she's a pretty big fan of your work. Why punish her zeal by making her click a link to read all your wisdom?

- People who use feed readers are pretty Web-savvy, which means that they aren't likely to click an ad and trap to zap the monkey. You won't be making any money off them with your ads anyway, so you should make it as easy as possible for them to read your stuff in the hope that they'll share it with their friends (who may be more inclined to zap the monkey).

So I recommend that you accept the default setting, Full Text. You'll thank me later.

Encoding

I also suggest that you accept the default encoding for pages and feeds (refer to Figure 5.20). Unless you have a strong reason to change the default, there isn't anything you need to know about this setting other than not to change it.

Discussion Settings

I've covered settings that govern how you post to your blog and how people read your blog, so what's left? Commenting, of course. Most of the options that you find in the Discussion Settings page, listed in the Settings section, are designed to reduce comment spam, allowing you to set a few simple parameters that apply to all comments on your blog.

Default article settings

The options in the Default Article Settings section apply to all of your posts, and as you see in **Figure 5.21**, they're all enabled when you install WordPress.

Figure 5.21 Article defaults are oddly named but useful.

Here's what the three options mean:

- **Attempt to Notify Any Blogs Linked to from the Article.** When you link to a blog post, WordPress attempts to notify the recipient of the link so that he can track who's linking to his post. This notification is known as a *pingback*. Then the linked blog can be configured to list all pingbacks (as well as *trackbacks*, which are basically the same) on a given post, thereby linking to your post on the post you linked to.

  Why would you want to turn this option off? As the setting's name itself notes, it slows posting slightly (though I've noticed hardly any slowness). The main reason for clearing this check box is to keep your blog private if you don't want to broadcast to the world the fact that you're blogging.

- **Allow Link Notifications from Other Blogs (Pingbacks and Trackbacks).** This feature tells your blog to accept, and display, the trackbacks and pingbacks that other blogs send to your blog.

> **note** If you decide to send out pingbacks, you should also accept them (which is only polite!).

- **Allow People to Post Comments on New Articles.** This setting enables or disables comments on posts at the system level. Out of the gate, WordPress assumes that you want people to comment on your posts, so it enables comments. If you'd rather not deal with comments, simply clear this check box.

    No matter what you set here, you also have the option of enabling or disabling comments on a per-post basis.

Other comment settings

The Other Comment Settings section (**Figure 5.22**) gives you greater control of who can comment on your blog and how those comments appear.

Figure 5.22 Comment settings apply to all comments on your blog.

These options are as follows:

- **Comment Author Must Fill out Name and E-Mail.** Checked by default, this setting prevents people from leaving a comment on your blog without providing a name and email address.

- **Users Must Be Registered and Logged in to Comment.** As I mention earlier in this chapter, WordPress can be configured to allow people to register for accounts on your blog. If you have this feature enabled, you can limit commenting to only those people who have accounts on your blog.

- **Automatically Close Comments on Articles Older Than *x* Days.**
  You can have WordPress disable comments on older posts automatically. Fill in a number here, and after that many days, readers will no
  longer be able to comment on a published post.

- **Enable Threaded (Nested) Comments *x* Levels Deep.** Threaded, or
  nested, comments are enabled by default with five levels of depth. This
  means that when someone replies to a comment thread, his reply will
  be indented and displayed below the comment he's replying to, up to
  five levels deep. You can choose to indent anywhere from two to ten
  levels, or you can have your comments displayed flat (all comments
  displayed with the same level of indentation) by disabling this feature.

- **Break Comments into Pages.** Here, you can specify whether you want
  to paginate your comments and, if so, how many comments to display
  on each page. You also set how the paginated comments are displayed:
  in chronological order (with the older comments listed at the top) or
  reverse chronological order (with the newer comments at the top).

- **Comment display.** Finally, you have to decide how you want the
  comments to be listed on each page: in reverse chronological order or
  chronological order.

Notification options

Now the email address you entered in "Email address" earlier in this chapter
comes into play. No doubt you'll be interested to know when people post a
comment on something you wrote. You can direct WordPress to email you,
the administrator, each and every time someone comments on any post, as
well as every time a comment is awaiting moderation (which I discuss later
in this chapter).

Choose one of the E-Mail Me Whenever options (**Figure 5.23** on the next page) to
be notified when

- **Anyone Posts a Comment.** Every comment on your blog, whether or
  not it's about a post you wrote, is emailed to you because you're the
  blog's administrator. This feature is great for keeping track of discus-
  sions on your blog, but if your blog starts getting a serious amount of
  comments, your inbox can get overwhelmed quickly.

- **A Comment Is Held for Moderation.** Another weapon against comment spam is comment moderation, which keeps all new incoming comments in a virtual holding pen. A comment can't be published on your blog until a user of your blog who plays the proper role logs in and approves it manually. (See Chapter 3 for more info on user roles.) If you enable this option, you get an email about every comment that's waiting for moderation and won't forget to approve legitimate comments. (Almost nothing is worse than commenting on someone's blog and never seeing that comment published.)

Figure 5.23 WordPress can keep you in the loop about comments.

Comment management

You can set some ground rules for comments in the next section of the Discussion Settings page: Before a Comment Appears (**Figure 5.24**). These options make managing comments a little easier by giving some comments a pass out of moderation (which means that they're posted without intervention by you or a designated user).

Before a comment appears
☐ An administrator must always approve the comment
☑ Comment author must have a previously approved comment

Figure 5.24 Comment spam is no fun, which is why you can set some minimum requirements for comments.

You can set either of these options:

- **An Administrator Must Always Approve the Comment.** You'll notice that this option isn't enabled by default. Who wants to spend all her time approving comments? But if you're a control freak, you can simply check this check box to make sure that no comments can appear on your blog without your approval.

- **Comment Author Must Have a Previously Approved Comment.**
  Rewarding good behavior is a tenet of our society, and the same holds true in WordPress. This option works on the theory that someone who had a previous comment approved by an administrator has earned the right to leave comments without moderation.

  If you enable this option, as soon as a preapproved commenter leaves another comment, it appears on the blog. This arrangement not only makes your commenter feel good, but also means that you have to spend less time moderating comments—and that's a good thing, as one famous blogger might say. (Yes, Martha Stewart has a blog, and she even runs WordPress.)

Comment moderation

I've mentioned comment moderation a few times already, and now I can give you a tour of the section that controls how comments end up in the moderation queue. Your blog is your kingdom, and you can rule it as you like. (Feel the power flow through you!) Setting a few options in the Comment Moderation section (**Figure 5.25**) helps you fight the scourge of comment spam.

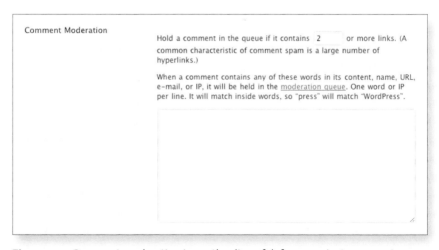

Comment Moderation

Hold a comment in the queue if it contains 2   or more links. (A common characteristic of comment spam is a large number of hyperlinks.)

When a comment contains any of these words in its content, name, URL, e-mail, or IP, it will be held in the moderation queue. One word or IP per line. It will match inside words, so "press" will match "WordPress".

Figure 5.25 Comment moderation is another line of defense against comment spam.

By default, a comment that has two or more links in it is held for moderation, even if the commenter in question is preapproved to leave comments (refer to the preceding section, "Comment management"). Why do this? Most comment spam contains a large number of links, usually to porn sites, which you probably aren't going to want on your blog. If you think legitimate users will be leaving more than two links in the body of their comments, you can adjust the number to your liking.

The large text box in this section lets you define some criteria that land a comment in moderation, no matter who leaves it. You can list words, IP (Internet Protocol) addresses, or particular links —one per line. If the terms you enter here appear in the name, email, URL, or text section of a comment, that comment is held in the moderation queue to wait for approval (or disapproval, as the case may be).

Comment blacklist

One step beyond comment moderation is the *comment blacklist*. To use this feature, just enter a list of banned items (such as URLs, IP addresses, terms, and email addresses) in the Comment Blacklist section (**Figure 5.26**). When any of these items is used in a comment, WordPress marks that comment as spam. Any comment that's marked as spam doesn't appear on your blog or even go into the moderation queue; it's held in your blog's spam queue, which is just like the Junk Mail folder in your email account.

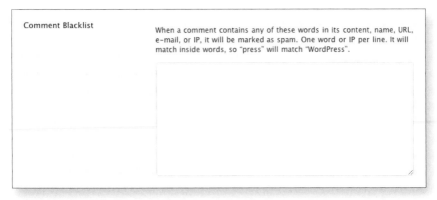

Figure 5.26 The time will come when you'll want to ban certain things, and the Comment Blacklist section is where you do that.

By default, WordPress doesn't give you a way to see what comments are in the spam queue. But if you activate the Akismet spam plug-in (see Chapter 11), you unlock several options related to spam comments that help you fight spam.

Avatar Settings

WordPress.org, along with WordPress.com, supports the Gravatar (Globally Recognized Avatar) service, another central service that complements WordPress (and yet another offering from Automattic).

Knowing your avatars from your gravatars

In case you aren't familiar with the concept on which this service is based, you need to start by getting familiar with avatars. An *avatar* is a digital artifact, such as a small picture, that represents you in cyberspace. Gravatar takes this concept one step further by allowing you to associate an avatar with an email address—thereby creating a *gravatar*. Whenever you comment from that email address on a blog that supports gravatars, your little icon shows up (**Figure 5.27**).

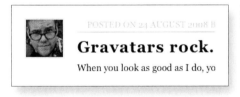

Figure 5.27 The author's gravatar. Handsome devil, ain't he?

> **tip** If you're interested in learning more about gravatars or setting up one for yourself, check out the Gravatar Web site at www.gravatar.com.

Enabling and disabling avatars

I'm willing to wager that gravatars are among those things that inspire strong feelings, both for and against. Some people think that gravatars liven up a drab blog and let people express their individuality; others think that gravatars are a silly waste of time. WordPress can accommodate either viewpoint. You can enable or disable gravatars with one click. If you don't want them on your blog, select the Don't Show Avatars radio button in the Avatar Display section (**Figure 5.28**), and skip to the "Privacy Settings" section later in this chapter.

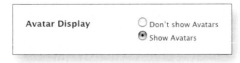

Figure 5.28
Avatars aren't for everyone.

Setting a default avatar

I know what you're thinking: "Scott, you have a great avatar!" Thanks— you're too kind. But what about folks who don't have avatars of their own? You can set a default avatar that WordPress will display for anyone who doesn't have a personal avatar. **Figure 5.29** shows the options in the Default Avatar section:

- Static images (Mystery Man and the Gravatar logo)

- Nothing at all (Blank)

- Avatars that WordPress generates randomly, based on the user's email address: Identicon (which looks like a bar code), Wavatar (a face based on a random geometric shape), or MonsterID (a little monster).

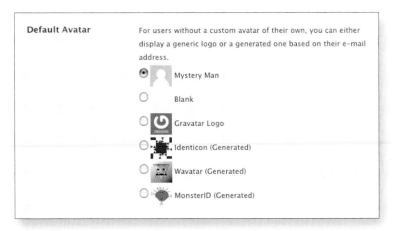

Figure 5.29 Not everyone has an avatar, so you can set a default avatar for those who aren't hip to the scene.

Avatar Ratings

Allowing people to post random pictures to your blog, even if they're in the form of tiny avatars, can be risky. A picture that one person thinks is appropriate may offend someone else. That's why WordPress has an avatar rating system that follows the familiar U.S. movie rating system (**Figure 5.30**).

Figure 5.30 If you don't want racy avatars on your blog, select the G radio button.

The ratings break down this way:

- **G.** Family friendly.

- **PG.** Appropriate for people 13 and older.

- **R.** Intended for mature audiences.

- **X.** Anything goes!

Unlike movie ratings, which are assigned by a governing board, avatar ratings are assigned by the very same person who created the avatar in the first place. The default rating is G. If you're open to having racier avatars gracing your blog, you can set this rating higher. (Don't worry—you can always change your mind later.)

Media Settings

The Media Settings page, listed in the Settings section, is where you decide how your blog will handle things like images and where it stores any kind of files associated with your blog (audio files, PDFs, or any other files you may want to host).

Image sizes

Whenever you upload a picture to WordPress, a couple of things happen:

- The file is saved in the appropriate directory. (If the directory doesn't exist, WordPress creates it.)

- Three thumbnails are created: small, medium, and large.

The Thumbnail Size and Medium Size settings (**Figure 5.31**) allow you to tell WordPress how large these thumbnails should be.

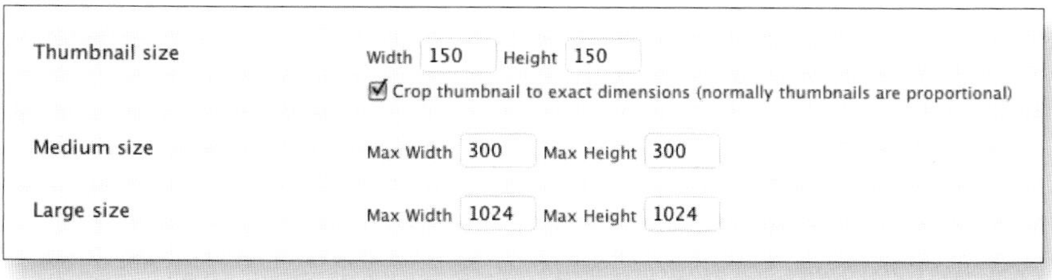

Thumbnail size	Width 150 Height 150
	☑ Crop thumbnail to exact dimensions (normally thumbnails are proportional)
Medium size	Max Width 300 Max Height 300
Large size	Max Width 1024 Max Height 1024

Figure 5.31 Thumbnail sizes are set systemwide.

The Crop Thumbnail to Exact Dimensions option, when enabled, means that the cropped thumbnail will have the exact dimensions you set in the Width and Height text boxes. (By default, thumbnails are 150 by 150 pixels.) If you don't want a square thumbnail, clear this check box, and enter the width and height values you prefer.

These settings come into play when you're inserting an image into a post. You have the choice of inserting the original picture or one of the thumbnails that WordPress creates based on these settings.

Embeds

Whenever you see a YouTube video on a site other YouTube, that video has been *embedded,* and you can do the same on your blog. The Embeds settings (**Figure 5.32**) make it very easy to embed video and other content in your blog.

Auto-Embeds, which is enabled by default, allows you to paste the URL of the object you want to embed (such as a YouTube video) and leave the rest to WordPress. When you publish the post, the content associated with the URL shows up in the post instead of the URL you actually entered.

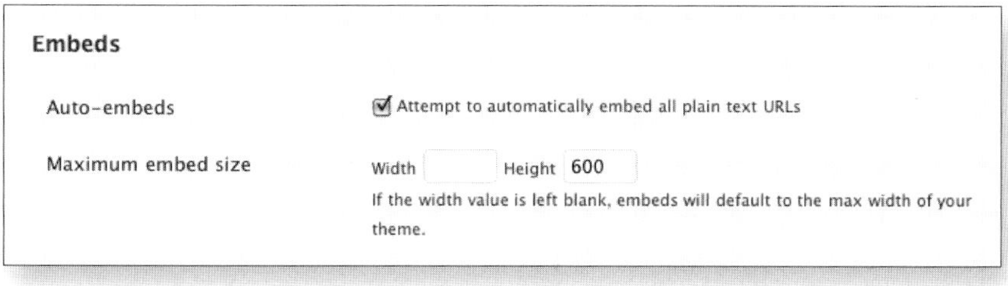

Embeds

Auto-embeds ☑ Attempt to automatically embed all plain text URLs

Maximum embed size Width [   ] Height [600]
If the width value is left blank, embeds will default to the max width of your theme.

Figure 5.32 Embeds are here to help you share content on your blog.

The Maximum Embed Size option ensures that an embedded asset won't mess up your blog's design by appearing too big.

File uploads

No doubt you'll be uploading lots of files to WordPress when you write posts. These files can include pictures, movies, and music, to name just a few options.

Uploads folder and file path

By default, WordPress stores the files you upload in a directory called wp-content/uploads, but you can change this setting in the Uploading Files section of the Media Settings page (**Figure 5.33**).

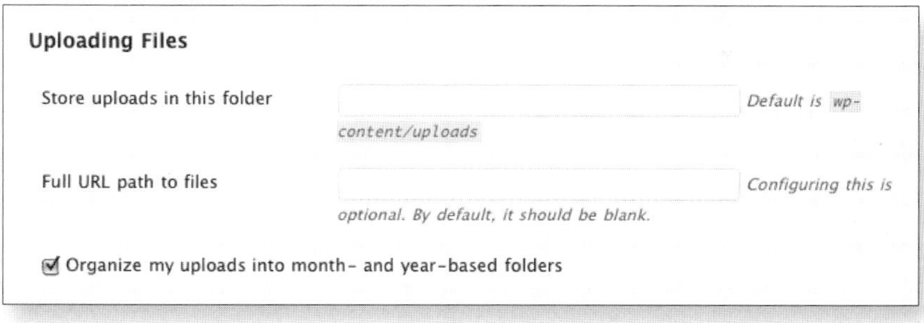

Uploading Files

Store uploads in this folder [   ] *Default is* wp-
content/uploads

Full URL path to files [   ] *Configuring this is*
optional. By default, it should be blank.

☑ Organize my uploads into month- and year-based folders

Figure 5.33 WordPress needs to know where to keep uploaded files and how you want them organized.

If you want to store files in a different location, just type it in the Store Uploads in This Folder text box. When you do, the Full URL Path to Files setting shouldn't be blank, as it is by default. Fill in the URL of the location you entered for the uploads folder, and you should be good to go.

Suppose that I want to store my files in a directory called files. I'd type **files** in the Store Uploads in This Folder text box and enter **http://www. wordpressforall.com/files** in the Full URL Path to Files text box.

Uploads organization

After you've been blogging for a while, you'll amass a large collection of random files on your server. WordPress organizes all uploaded files in monthly and annual folders.

Suppose that on August 12, 2008, you uploaded a file called scott.gif. WordPress checks your uploads folder for that file. If a folder called 2008 doesn't exist, WordPress creates it, as well as a folder called 08, which it places inside the 2008 folder. Then it places the image you uploaded inside the 08 folder. The URL for this image would be something like this:

http://www.wordpressforall.com/files/2008/08/scott.gif

If you prefer, you can clear the organization check box (refer to Figure 5.33) to keep your files as messy as you like.

Privacy Settings

Think back to when you installed WordPress (lo, these many pages ago; flip back to Chapter 2). Do you recall that the installer asked you whether you wanted your blog to be listed with search engines (such as Google)? If you ever change your mind about that choice, you can easily set the appropriate Site Visibility setting in the Privacy Settings section of the Settings page (**Figure 5.34**).

Figure 5.34 Search engines aren't all-seeing. You can opt out of them by making your site "invisible."

note Blocking search engines won't stop people from loading your site; they just won't be able to find the site easily.

Permalink Settings

The Internet is built on the concept of linking. You link to my blog, I link to yours, and everyone's happy. The unspoken agreement in linking is that link locations won't change. Each of your individual posts has a URL associated with it; this URL is called a *permalink*. This permalink is meant to be permanent so that people can always find your post, no matter when they visit that link.

Structure of a permalink

By default, a blog's URL structure looks like this:

http://www.wordpressforall.com/?p=11

The first part is the blog's URL (in this example, www.wordpressforall.com). After the slash (/) is ?p=, which is how PHP handles URL variables (in this case, p stands for *post*). The number is the POST ID variable of the post in question. Databases such as MySQL can easily remember things based on variables like POST ID, but we humans are made of different stuff. No one has ever said to me, "Hey, Scott, I really enjoyed Post 243 on your blog the other day."

People aren't the only things that are at a disadvantage with the default WordPress URL structure: The URLs aren't very friendly to search engines either. The more descriptive your permalinks are, the better a search engine can index them, resulting in more people being able to find your blog.

Permalinks are important, which is why WordPress devotes a whole section of settings to them. Before I get into the various kinds of permalinks you can set up for your blog, however, I need to discuss how they work on a technical level.

How permalinks work

WordPress supports various types of permalinks by using the `mod_rewrite` module for Apache—a piece of software known as a Web server. Your Web host most likely is using Apache because the software is both very popular and free (funny how that works). Functionality can be added to Apache via modules, one of which is `mod_rewrite`, which enables Apache to rewrite URLs on the fly. This module is important for purposes of this discussion because no matter which permalink structure you choose, WordPress uses the URL with the POST ID in it to find your post. The mod_rewrite module knows how to map one URL that is easy to remember to another URL based on rules.

The mod_rewrite rules can become complicated quickly, but WordPress takes care of writing the rules for you, so don't worry about them. Check your Web host's documentation, however, to make sure that its servers support mod_rewrite.

tip **If you're interested to see the mod_rewrite rules, look for a file called .htaccess. Notice the leading dot, which in many operating systems means that the file is hidden. Check your FTP program's preferences, and make sure that it's set to show you invisible files. Open the file in a text editor, but don't change anything. You wouldn't want to break your blog's URL structure.**

Permalink structure options

When you've made sure that mod_rewrite is available to you, go ahead and pick your permalink structure in the Common Settings section (**Figure 5.35**).

Common settings	
⦿ Default	http://www.ipadbungalow.com/?p=123
○ Day and name	http://www.ipadbungalow.com/2010/08/21/sample-post/
○ Month and name	http://www.ipadbungalow.com/2010/08/sample-post/
○ Numeric	http://www.ipadbungalow.com/archives/123
○ Custom Structure	

Figure 5.35 The various permalink structures that WordPress offers. You can make a custom structure if none of these suits you.

WordPress has five options for permalinks. I discuss them all in the following sections.

Default

The default structure isn't very friendly, as you see in Figure 5.35.

Day and Name

This option creates a permalink based on a combination of the date of the post and the post title. Suppose that a post called "WordPress for All launches" was posted August 18, 2008. If you choose the Day and Name option, you get this permalink:

http://www.wordpressforall.com/2008/08/18/wordpress-for-all-launches/

Notice that the title in the link is all lowercase. If I'd used a non-URL-friendly character such as an apostrophe (') or percent sign (%) in the title, WordPress would have stripped that character out so that the link will work in Web browsers.

Month and Name

This option drops the day from the URL for a shorter permalink, such as this:

http://www.wordpressforall.com/2008/08/wordpress-for-all-launches/

 tip   **Some people like shorter permalinks because they're easier to type.**

Numeric

The Numeric option is even shorter, creating a permalink like this:

http://www.wordpressforall.com/archives/11

This permalink structure brings back your old friend POST ID but presents it in a way that is a little less cryptic than ?p=11.

Custom Structure

Whenever you select one of the first four permalink structures, the Custom Structure text box is populated automatically. When you select Day and Name, for example, this appears in the text box:

/%year%/%monthnum%/%day%/%postname%/

All permalink structures are built from these permalink tags. You can build your very own custom permalink structure (see the nearby sidebar) by mixing and matching tags.

tip For a full list of tags that you can use in your WordPress permalink structure, visit this page of the WordPress Codex: http://codex. wordpress.org/Using_Permalinks#Structure_Tags.

Creating Custom Permalinks

Want to create a few custom permalink structures, just for fun? Sure you do.

If you use the author tag (**%author%**) like so

/%author%/%year%/%postname%/

you get a permalink that features the author's user name, the year, and the post name (and you can add other units of time if you like):

http://www.wordpressforall.com/scott/2008/wordpress-for-all-launches/

You don't have to limit yourself to the WordPress tags. Here, I've started my custom structure with the word **permalink**:

/permalink/%year%/%monthnum%/%postname%/

That structure generates this permalink:

http://www.wordpressforall.com/permalink/2008/08/wordpress-for-all-launches/

You can also add text to the end of tags to add extensions. If you ever plan on migrating your WordPress blog to a series of static HTML files, this permalink will save you some broken links:

/permalink/%postname%.html

See that `.html` at the end? It makes the permalink look like this:

http://www.wordpressforall.com/permalink/wordpress-for-all-launches.html

WordPress is still building this page dynamically, but now you have the option of creating a static HTML version of this page, and links won't break. Nifty, huh?

Category and tag permalinks

You have two ways to organize your content in WordPress: tags and categories. I get into the differences between the two in Chapter 6, but suffice it to say that both options exist. You can change the way the permalinks associated with categories and tags work by setting their *base phrase*—a word that's used after your blog's URL in the tag/category URL as the foundation for the link.

By default, the permalink that lists all posts categorized as wordpress on my blog looks like this:

http://www.wordpressforall.com/category/wordpress/

Similarly, the permalink for anything tagged blogging looks like this:

http://www.wordpressforall.com/tag/blogging/

If you leave the Category Base and Tag Base text boxes blank in the Optional section (**Figure 5.36**), WordPress uses these defaults.

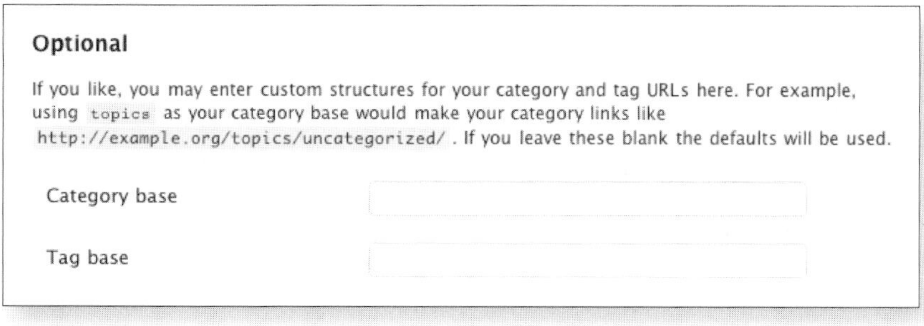

Figure 5.36 Categories and tags also have permalinks, and you can change their base phrases here.

If you want your categories to be called subjects instead, however, type **subject** in the Category Base text box, and click Save. Now the permalink looks like this:

http://www.wordpressforall.com/subject/wordpress/

You can mix and match default tag bases and custom category bases with no problem.

6

Preparing to Post

Building a good blog post is all about having good content. WordPress won't make you a better blogger, but if you know how to format your post, you can at least appear to know what you're doing. (I've been coasting along using this strategy for most of my life.) In this chapter, I show you how to set up a WordPress post like a pro, but I leave the actual content up to you.

WordPress tries to get out of your way so as to make writing posts easy. When you click the big New Post button at the top of every WordPress admin screen (**Figure 6.1**), WordPress displays the Posts screen.

Figure 6.1 The New Post button is waiting for you to click it.

You'll notice that the Posts entry in the left navigation bar has expanded and offers four options: Posts, Add New, Categories, and Post Tags (**Figure 6.2**). I cover each of these options in turn.

Figure 6.2 The Posts options.

Breaking Down the Elements of a Post

No matter what blogging system you use, posts always have three elements: a title, a body, and an author. WordPress adds a few more things to the mix, but the basics are the same. The rest of this chapter goes through the various sections of the Add New Post screen in order.

Title

Titles are like headlines in a newspaper. A good title makes you want to read the post, makes you curious, and gives you a sense of what you're about to read. Depending on your permalink structure, your titles may also be used in the permalinks themselves. (Refer to Chapter 5 for more info on permalinks.)

The permalink for your post is generated after the first automatic save. As you write a post, WordPress automatically saves at certain intervals to ensure that if your browser crashes or you're somehow disconnected from WordPress, your entire post isn't lost.

Right below the title you see, in a light font, the word *Permalink* followed by the URL of the permalink (**Figure 6.3**). The last section of the permalink is high-lighted. This part, called the *slug*, generally is based on the title of the post.

Figure 6.3 A very creative title for a blog post, don't you think? Notice the permalink below the title.

If you don't like the slug, just click the Edit button; change the slug displayed in the text box (**Figure 6.4**) to something you do like; and click OK. Now you have an improved permalink that says exactly what you want.

Permalink: http://www.ipadbungalow.com/2010/08/23/ `latin-blogging-for-fun` / (OK) Cancel

Figure 6.4 Editing a post's permalink is easy.

note Titles, like all other fields in a post, are optional.

Body

The meat of posting happens in the body, which you write in the Add New Post screen. You have lots of options in this screen, and you can use as many or as few of them as you like. (One great thing about WordPress is that it offers loads of features but doesn't force you to use them.)

When posting, you can choose between two tabs at the very top of the post body:

- **Visual.** Click this tab to write your posts with the Visual Editor.

- **HTML.** Click this tab to write in straight HTML code.

You can switch back and forth between the two options easily. The Visual and HTML areas have different features, so I look at them separately in the following sections.

At the bottom of the body section is some information about the post itself: who last edited the post and when, when the draft was saved, and how many words are in the post.

Composing and Formatting a Post

Writing is a very personal activity, and every writer has a list of particular tools, pens, notebooks, and the like that he or she prefers. Writing in your WordPress blog is just like jotting something down in your favorite note-book, except that you have no notebook, and you aren't actually committing ink (or graphite) to paper. WordPress gives you two different ways to interact with the Add New Post screen: the Visual Editor and HTML view. Both features allow you to write and format a post—just in different ways. Choose whichever feature you're more comfortable with.

Writing with the Visual Editor

WordPress uses an open-source visual HTML editor called *TinyMCE*. All the features listed in this section are available in any product that uses TinyMCE.

 note   You can find out more about this JavaScript marvel by visiting the TinyMCE Web site (http://tinymce.moxiecode.com).

The Visual Editor (**Figure 6.5**) takes care of all the code behind the formatting of your words. If you're not interested in learning how to hand-code HTML, you'll want to use this editor to post to your blog. The following sections cover the Visual Editor's buttons and show you what they do.

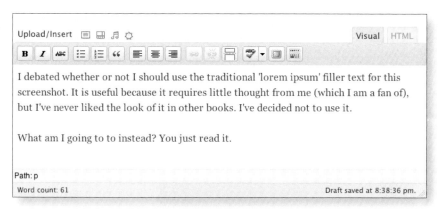

Figure 6.5 Composing a post in the Visual Editor.

 tip   When you hover your mouse pointer over a button in the Visual Editor, a tool tip pops up, displaying the keyboard shortcut for that button.

Formatting toolbars: Top row

No matter which view you use, you'll see a toolbar at the top of the editing form. Each toolbar button formats your post in one way or another. This section covers the top toolbar.

Sometimes you want a word or phrase to stand out, and one of the best ways to achieve that goal is to boldface that text. Select whatever words you want to boldface; then click the Bold button. The selected words will be bold in the editor window and in the post as well.

Italics are another way of emphasizing your words, and as you might guess, the Italic button applies that format. Select the words you want to italicize, click the button, and you're done.

The Strikethrough button is a great way to acknowledge a mistake without removing the erroneous information. ~~My face~~ Strikethrough is also used for comedic effect in many cases.

The next two buttons let you create lists. To create a bulleted list (also known as an *unordered list*), click the leftmost of these two buttons; then select some text or an image to be your first list item. WordPress inserts a bullet, and when you press Enter or Return, you can add another item to the list. (Pressing Enter or Return twice ends the list so that you can go back to writing normally.) A numbered (or *ordered*) list works the same way but creates a list whose items are numbered (as you may have suspected from the name).

Quoting people is fairly common in the blogosphere, but how do you note that the relevant section of your post is a quote from elsewhere? Block quotes are the answer. When you select some text and click the Block Quote button, WordPress creates a block quote and populates it with the selected text. Depending on the styling of your blog, block quotes can appear in a variety of ways. Usually, a block quote is indented and shown with a different-colored background, so that there's no doubt in the reader's mind that this section is a quote. (Always credit your sources, kids. No one likes a plagiarist.)

The next three buttons—Left, Center, and Right— allow you to align the text of your post. You can use whichever option you want, but WordPress defaults to left-aligned text.

I'll wager that you'll use this set of buttons most. The button with the links of chain on it turns any selected word or phrase into a hyperlink. Clicking this button brings up the Insert/Edit Link dialog box (**Figure 6.6**), where you set the following options:

- **Link URL.** This text box provides the destination of the link (a URL of some kind).

- **Target.** The Target setting specifies where the link opens in the user's Web browser. You can have the link open in the same browser window or in a new one.

- **Title.** The title of the link shows up when someone hovers a mouse pointer over the link or accesses your site with a text browser.

- **Class.** Class is a styling option that you can use, in conjunction with some CSS (Cascading Style Sheets), to apply formatting to your links. If you don't know what CSS is, chances are that you can ignore this option.

Figure 6.6 The Insert/Edit Link dialog box allows you to insert a new link or edit an existing one.

If you want to change any of these values for an existing link, click the Hyperlink button again; the dialog box shows you the current values, and you can change them however you want.

Back in the Visual Editor toolbar, click the button with the broken chain to remove the linking code from the selected word. The word itself isn't deleted—just the code that makes it a link.

It's commonplace to see a Read More link at the bottom of blog posts nowadays. The idea is that you should cut longer blog posts into two sections so that your blog's front page isn't overwhelmed by your epic post about Bayesian economics and its effect on lobster prices in central Utah. Clicking this button inserts a `<!--more-->` tag and displays a dotted line across the posting field in the Add New Post screen. Anything before the dotted line is displayed on the front page of your blog. At the end of that section is a Read More link. Clicking the Read More link takes you to the entries page, which contains the full text of the post (including everything after the dotted line in the Add New Post screen).

I don't know about you, but spell checkers have ruined what little spelling ability I have (just ask my editors). WordPress furthers my spelling decline by offering spell check. Clicking the Spell Check button enables it; clicking the button again disables it. Misspelled words are underlined in red; click an underlined word to see a list of suggested spellings, as well as options to ignore this occurrence of the word or all occurrences in the entire post.

Full-screen mode is all the rage in desktop word processors. It allows you to block out all distractions and concentrate on the work at hand: crafting memorable words for your readers. The Full Screen button expands the posting field to occupy your entire screen. Click the button again to toggle back to normal view.

The very last button in the top toolbar is interesting, because it isn't the last button at all. Clicking the kitchen-sink button (yes, that's the real name) reveals a second toolbar that's hidden from view by default (**Figure 6.7**).

Figure 6.7 The second toolbar is usually hidden away. Clicking the kitchen-sink button reveals it.

Formatting toolbars: Bottom row

This second toolbar offers some functionality that you probably won't need for every post but that may come in handy from time to time. WordPress remembers whether you've displayed this extra toolbar, so if you find yourself using one of these features, you can keep the toolbar on display.

Here are the buttons and what they do:

Paragraph ▾ The Format drop-down menu gives you access to various text-formatting options. Select the text you want to format and choose an option from the drop-down menu: Paragraph, Preformatted, a variety of heading options, and so on.

U Because links are traditionally underlined, people avoid underlining text for any other reason. That being said, you can click this button to underline selected text.

☰ Justified text isn't too common on the Web, but if you want all your lines to be the same width, select the text and click this button.

A ▾ By default, your blog's theme (see Chapter 12) determines the color of the text in your posts. If you want to change the color of selected text, this button gives you access to all the colors of the rainbow. Click the down arrow on the button to display a grid of colors (**Figure 6.8**).

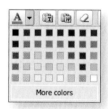

Figure 6.8 You have a full range of colors at your fingertips.

If these choices aren't enough, view even more color options by clicking More Colors at the bottom of the grid. The More Colors screen gives you three options for finding just the right color: Color Picker, which shows a rainbow of colors that you can choose among; Palette, which offers up an expanded grid of colors; and Named, which gives you the opportunity to choose one of the so-called Web-safe colors. Each option displays the hex code for the selected color. (*Hex codes* are used in HTML to tell Web browsers what color to display.) If you know the hex code of the color you're after, you can enter it directly in the box labeled Color.

T Copying and pasting text usually is straightforward, but sometimes when you copy text, you also copy unwanted formatting. Click the Paste As Plain Text button to strip out all the formatting and paste only the text. Paste the text in the dialog box that pops up after you click the button (**Figure 6.9**), check or clear the Keep Linebreaks check box, and then click the Insert button to paste the text into your post.

Figure 6.9
The Paste As Plain Text
dialog box.

The Paste from Word button also displays a dialog box for your pasted text (**Figure 6.10**). It works the same way as the Paste As Plain Text dialog box (see the preceding paragraph), but instead of stripping out Microsoft Word formatting, it makes that formatting HTML-friendly. This feature is very useful if you compose your posts in Word with lots of text formatting and don't want to delete the Word-specific markup that gets copied along with your text.

Figure 6.10
The Paste from Word
dialog box.

The Remove Formatting button strips all formatting out of the selected text.

The Insert/Edit Embedded Media button deals specifically with media files (QuickTime, Adobe Flash, Windows Media, and Real Media files) that you want to embed in your post. The various options for each file type are beyond the scope of this book; I recommend that you poke around the Advanced tab of the media screen and see what works best for you.

Custom characters (also known as *special characters* and *HTML entities*) are characters that have special HTML codes associated with them to ensure that they show up correctly in Web browsers. Click this button to open the Select Custom Character dialog box (**Figure 6.11**); then select the character you're interested in to insert it into your post, all without having to worry about the code.

Figure 6.11 The custom-character picker.

The Outdent and Indent buttons outdent and indent paragraphs, respectively. Position the insertion point where you want to apply the formatting, and click the appropriate button.

The Undo button allows you to undo an action such as deleting a word or pasting the wrong text. If you decide that you really did like the post the way it was before, click the Redo button. Your post is as it was.

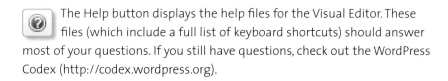 The Help button displays the help files for the Visual Editor. These files (which include a full list of keyboard shortcuts) should answer most of your questions. If you still have questions, check out the WordPress Codex (http://codex.wordpress.org).

Writing in HTML view

You may want to use HTML view instead when you write your posts, for a couple of reasons:

- You're faster at hand-coding than you are at selecting text and clicking formatting buttons.

- You want to enter some code from a third-party Web site (such as Digg or YouTube).

Any code that you enter in a post via the Visual Editor is treated as text, not as code. This means that the code is displayed just as you entered it—but doesn't execute and call up a video or what have you. Solving this problem is simple: Just click the HTML tab (**Figure 6.12**) and paste your code in the resulting HTML window.

Figure 6.12 Switching between the Visual Editor and HTML view is as simple as clicking a tab.

HTML view allows you to enter code by hand, but it also has a row of buttons that generate code for you (to save time). This view offers some, but not all, of the Visual Editor's functionality. A big difference is that you don't need to select text for the buttons in HTML view to work. Because the buttons in HTML view enter HTML code, which is tag-based, clicking a button inserts the appropriate opening tag into the entry. Click the button again to insert the closing tag at the insertion-point location in the post.

Following are the HTML-view buttons and what they do.

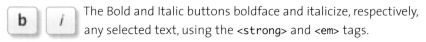 The Bold and Italic buttons boldface and italicize, respectively, any selected text, using the `<strong>` and `<em>` tags.

The Link button creates a link, using the selected word as the link's text. When you click this button, a window pops up; enter the appropriate URL in this window, and you're good to go.

b-quote   The B-Quote button is the Block Quote button; it does the same thing as its counterpart in the Visual Editor (refer to "Formatting toolbars: Top row" earlier in this chapter).

del ins   The Del and Ins buttons flag text that has been deleted from your post or added to your post, respectively. Text between the `<del>` tags is displayed in strikethrough; text between the `<ins>` tags looks like a link (depending on the style of your blog).

img   The Img button allows you to insert an image, as long as you know the URL of the image. In "Adding Media to a Post" later in this chapter, though, I cover an easier way to insert images (assuming that they are uploaded to your WordPress blog).

ul ol li   The tags that create lists are `<ul>` (unordered, or bulleted), `<ol>` (ordered, or numbered), and `<li>` (list item, used between the `<ul>` and `<ol>` tags). Click the appropriate buttons to insert these tags.

code   If you plan on blogging about technical subjects, you'll want to know about the Code button. This button inserts the `<code>` tag, which displays text in a monospace font (`like this`), signifying that it's code of some sort.

more   The More button inserts a Read More link (refer to "Formatting toolbars: Top row" earlier in this chapter). Any text before the `<more>` tag is displayed on the front page of your blog; everything after it appears only on the post's page.

lookup   The Lookup button doesn't insert anything into your post. Rather, it looks up the selected word at Answers.com, which can be fun, but I haven't found this particular function to be all that useful.

close tags   The Close Tags button, as you might expect, closes any open HTML tags. This functionality isn't perfect, though; you should double-check the tags it closes to ensure that they're handled properly.

Adding Media to a Post

A good blog post starts with text, which you now know how to manipulate in WordPress, but also includes other kinds of media. Adding images, movies, audio files, PDFs, and many more media types to your posts is easy and even fun.

You use the Upload/Insert section of the Add New Post screen (**Figure 6.13**) to...well, add media to your posts or pages. The four icons represent images, movies, audio files, and all other media files.

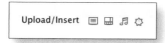

Figure 6.13 The Add Media options let you spiff up your posts with pictures, videos, and other files.

Clicking an icon brings up an appropriate uploader for the media type in question (**Figure 6.14**).

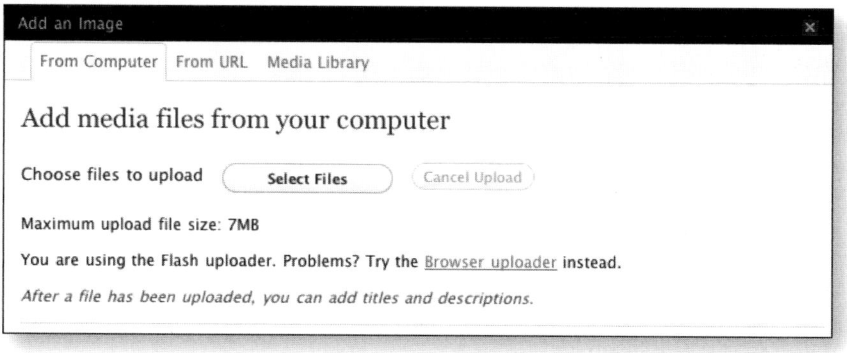

Figure 6.14 Choose a file to upload.

Adding images

The first icon in the Add Media section—the one that looks like a picture frame—adds images to your post. When you click that icon, an uploader page pops up (refer to Figure 6.14). You can upload a picture (or set of pictures) from your computer, insert a picture from the Web by clicking the From URL tab, or select an image you have in your Media Library.

I cover each method in the following sections.

Just Say No to Hotlinking

Insert pictures from the Web with caution. Use this method only for pictures that you own and host yourself or for images that are hosted by a large picture-hosting site (such as Flickr).

Posting images from other people's blogs is called *hotlinking* and generally isn't looked upon kindly. Every time someone reads your blog post with a hotlinked picture in it, the person who actually hosts that picture has to pay for the bandwidth your reader uses to view it.

Inserting an image from a URL

If you're sure that you can use this method (refer to the nearby sidebar "Just Say No to Hotlinking"), click the From URL tab in the uploader page. You need to provide a few pieces of information:

- **Image URL.** Enter the URL of the image you want to insert. After you enter something in this text box, WordPress tries to find an image at the URL you provided (assuming that you're connected to the Internet). Depending on what it finds, WordPress displays a green check mark next to the Source text box if the image is reachable or a red X if the image can't be retrieved.

- **Image Title.** The image title, which is required, is used in the TITLE attribute of the image. This attribute is commonly used to describe an element on a Web page, so make sure that your title is appropriate.

- **Alternate Text.** Not everyone can see images on the Web, and not everyone who can see them loads images. Alternate Text exists so that you can give a text description of the image for accessibility reasons.

- **Image Caption.** A caption serves double duty. Some themes display the text you enter here below the image and also use it to populate the image's <alt> tag. (The <alt> tag contains the text that you want to show up in the user's browser when the image can't be displayed or the person who's looking at your site is using a text-only browser.)

- **Alignment.** This setting determines how text flows around your image. None causes the image to sit above the text. Left aligns the picture to the left side of the post, and the text flows around it. Center places the image in the center of the post, and text doesn't flow around the image. Right is the opposite of Left.

- **Link Image To.** Entering a URL in the Link URL text box turns the picture you're inserting into a link to said URL. You can enter any URL you want in this box or click the Link to Image button, which populates the text box with the URL of the image itself (which will be the same as the Source setting). This feature is useful if you plan to insert a thumbnail of a picture. People can click the thumbnail to see the image full size.

When you have the settings to your liking (**Figure 6.15**), just click the Insert into Post button. WordPress inserts the image into the post at the location of the insertion point.

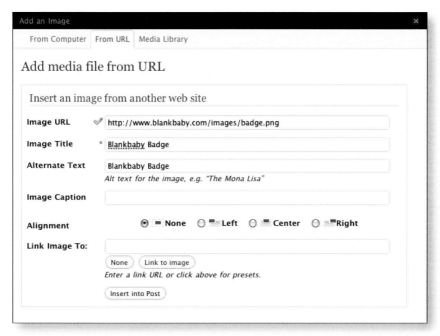

Figure 6.15 Notice the check mark next to the Image URL text box; it means that WordPress found the image.

Uploading an image from your computer

If you want to upload an image from your computer to your blog, which means that you'll be hosting the image on your server, you have to use a WordPress uploader. The default uploader uses the Flash plug-in from Adobe. If you're not a fan of Flash or if your browser doesn't support it, you can click the Browser Uploader link at the top of the uploader page instead (refer to Figure 6.14). The browser uploader doesn't require plug-ins and should work on most systems.

The Flash uploader has one feature that the browser uploader lacks: a progress bar. This bar charts the upload process as well as the generation of thumbnails (during which process the progress bar displays the word *Crunching*). You can upload multiple files with either uploader, so if you don't care about the progress bar, either option will suit your needs.

To upload images from your computer, follow these steps:

1. Click the From Computer tab of the uploader page.

2. Click the Select Files button.

   A file browser appears.

3. Select the photos you want to upload from your computer.

 tip   Holding down the Shift key while you click a bunch of contiguous files allows you to select and upload all those images at the same time. You can also Ctrl-click (or, on the Mac, Control-click) to select noncontiguous files in the same folder.

4. When you have the correct images selected, click Open.

   WordPress starts uploading the files.

When an image is uploaded, the image properties page automatically opens and displays many of the same settings that it displays for images from the Web, which I cover in the preceding section (**Figure 6.16**).

Figure 6.16 After an image has been uploaded from your computer, you can set a few options for it.

Most of the settings do the same things, but here are the differences:

- **Title.** Again, the title is required. This time, in addition to setting the TITLE attribute of this image, the title identifies this image in your blog's Media Library, which I cover in "Using Media Library" later in this chapter.

- **Description.** Another field that shows up in Media Library when you're searching for a picture, Description is also used in galleries (which I cover in the next section).

- **Link URL.** You can set one of three options for the link URL: None, File URL, or Post URL.

  None is what you want to click if you don't want this image to be a link to anything.

  File URL allows you to set a direct link to the file on your server. If you upload an image called blogsarecool.jpg, that URL would look like this:

  http://*www.yourblog.com/yourWordPressfolder*/wp-content/ uploads/2008/08/blogsarecool.jpg

  Post URL isn't the permalink of the post itself but a permalink to the image. (For more information on permalinks, flip back to Chapter 5.) When you upload an image to a post, that image is attached to the post, essentially creating a subpost that contains only the uploaded image. The Post URL setting refers to this subpost. This subpost is just like any other post in your blog, in that people can link to it and leave comments. You can click the Post URL button and enter any URL you want to use.

- **Size.** If you're reading the chapters of this book in order, you may recall a setting in Chapter 5 that affects the sizes of thumbnails of uploaded images. This option is where that setting pays off. You can insert the picture at the size of the original (Full Size), or you can insert it by using the thumbnail options: Thumbnail, Medium, or Large.

tip   **If, just as you click the Insert into Post button, you realize that the image you're working with isn't right, fear not! You can delete it right from the uploader page. Click the Delete link, and WordPress warns you that you're about to delete the picture you just uploaded. Click Continue, and the picture is gone.**

The final difference is the Use As Featured Image link at the bottom of the image properties page. Any of your posts can have one featured image associated with it. Think of the featured image as being a thumbnail of the post. Some themes use the featured image to identify recent posts or to highlight interesting posts. When you click this link, WordPress creates a thumbnail of the image and sets that thumbnail as the post's featured image.

Working with galleries

Images are associated with the posts into which they are inserted, which allows you to create a gallery of images easily. When you upload multiple files to the same post, you'll notice that a Gallery tab appears at the top of the uploader page, with a number next to it in parentheses (**Figure 6.17**). That number is the number of pictures in the gallery associated with the post. You can insert images individually or insert multiple images as a gallery.

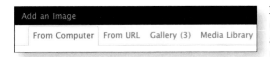

Figure 6.17 Image files that are uploaded through a post are attached to that post and automatically added to a gallery.

Why would you want to insert images as a gallery? This method gives you a little more control of how the images are displayed.

In this section, I give you a tour of the Gallery tab.

Reordering gallery images

Figure 6.18 shows seven pictures associated with a post, listed in the Gallery tab in the order in which they appear in the gallery.

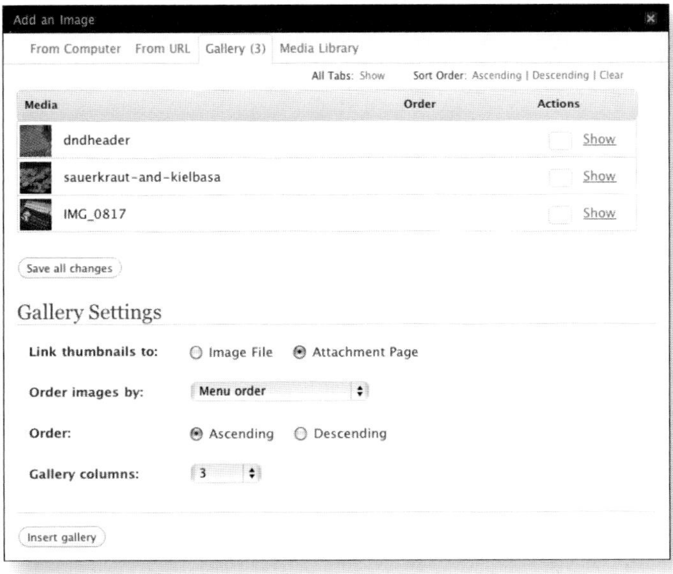

Figure 6.18 The gallery interface lists all the files that have been uploaded to this post.

If you want to change the order, you can do that in three ways:

- Use the sort-order options at the top of the image list. You can sort your pictures in ascending or descending alphabetical order (based on their file names). Click the Clear link to remove any and all ordering.

- Click and drag the picture you want to move to a different position. The other pictures move to new places, and the gallery is reordered. Notice that WordPress automatically fills in the Order column after you drop an image into a new position (**Figure 6.19**).

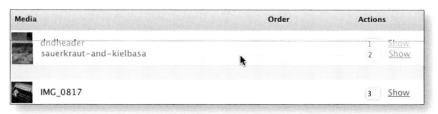

Media	Order	Actions
dndheader	1	Show
sauerkraut-and-kielbasa	2	Show
IMG_0817	3	Show

Figure 6.19 If you want to change the order of a picture in the gallery, you can drag the picture or type an new ordinal number in the picture's Order column.

- Setting the Order column by hand also reorders the gallery. Lower numbers appear before higher numbers.

note **If you have an image file that's attached to the post but don't want it to show up in the gallery, leave its Order column blank.**

Clicking a Show link (next to the Order column) expands the settings for the selected image (**Figure 6.20**). You can change the title, caption, description, or link URL of the image; you can also insert the image into a post by itself.

Click the Save All Changes button in the Gallery tab (refer to Figure 6.18) to save both the order and the changes that you made for each image. When your galley is ready to go, click the Insert Gallery into Post button to insert the gallery short code—[gallery]—into your post. This code tells WordPress to display your gallery in that post.

Figure 6.20 When you click a Show link in the Gallery tab, you get some options to edit and can insert the file directly into a post.

Configuring gallery settings

Right below the images included in the gallery is the Gallery Settings section (refer to Figure 6.18). This section's settings are

- **Link Thumbnails To.** Every image in a gallery links to something— either the image file itself or an attachment page. An *attachment page* is a special page on your blog that shows only the image in question. You can decide where you want your images to link by picking one option or the other here.

- **Order Images By.** This drop-down menu lists four sorting options for your gallery. The default is Menu Order, which is the order you set in the media list; the other three are By Title, Date/Time the Image Was Taken, and Random.

- **Order.** This option is pretty straightforward. You just set the criteria for the ordering: ascending or descending.

- **Gallery Columns.** By default, galleries display three images across in each row. You're not limited to three rows, though; you can have as few as two and as many as nine by making a different choice from this drop-down menu.

> **note** Keep in mind that your blog's theme may have styling code that works best with a certain number of columns. (I discuss themes in Chapters 12 and 13.)

When you're happy with the gallery settings, click the Insert Gallery button, and your gallery appears in the post. If you clicked the Visual tab in the Add New Post screen (refer to "Writing with the Visual Editor" earlier in this chapter), you'll see the Gallery icon (**Figure 6.21**). When you hover over this icon with your mouse, two other icons appear. Clicking the first icon allows you to edit the gallery (see "Editing image settings" later in this chapter), and clicking the second icon (a red circle with a slash through it) removes the gallery from the post.

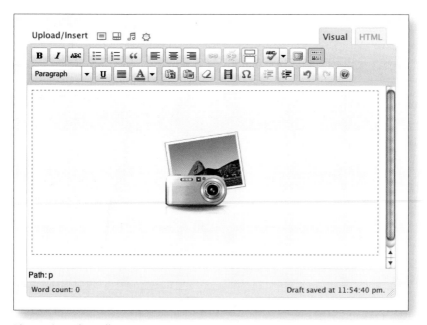

Figure 6.21 The gallery icon in a post.

[gallery] short code

Clicking the HTML tab of the Add New Post screen reveals that after all that work, all that is inserted into your post is something that looks like this: [gallery]. This code is called *short code,* which is a snippet of text that WordPress will replace dynamically with something else (in this case, your gallery).

You can set a few options for the short code that aren't available in the gallery interface itself:

- Galleries automatically show the thumbnails of the images, which makes sense, because you're showing several images in a small space. If you'd rather display one of the other sizes (such as Medium or Full Size; refer to "Uploading an image from your computer" earlier in this chapter), you can do so by adding size="" to the tag. If you want to show full-size images, use this code:

  [gallery size="full"]

  For medium images, use this code:

  [gallery size="medium"]

- Because images that are uploaded to a post are associated with that post, the gallery short code assumes that you want to include the images attached to the post in which the short code is used. If you want to use the same gallery in a different post, but you don't want to upload all those pictures again, you can use the id option. First, though, you need to know the POST ID of the post associated with the pictures (see the nearby note). After you get the POST ID, enter the short code like so:

  [galley id="52"]

  The POST ID is displayed in the URL of the post form. Just look for post. php?post=52&action=edit. The number after the first equal sign is the POST ID.

Viewing a gallery on your Web site

After you publish your post, the gallery is live on your site (**Figure 6.22**).

Figure 6.22 A post with a gallery, displayed in the default WordPress theme.

Clicking one of the pictures takes you to that picture's page, which shows the picture's title, the picture at whatever size you set (the default is medium), the description (if it has one), and the next and previous pictures in the gallery. Clicking the picture in this page takes you to the full-size version of the image.

Editing image settings

You know how to get images into your posts now. But what if you want to change an image's settings? You don't have to delete it and start from scratch. If you move your mouse pointer over an image in a post that you're editing or writing, the two icons shown in **Figure 6.23** appear.

Figure 6.23 Click the landscape icon to edit the picture's settings or the "prohibited" symbol to remove the picture from the post.

The red circle with a line through it—the universal "prohibited" symbol—deletes the image from your post. It doesn't delete the image itself, though; the image still exists in your images folder.

The other icon, which looks like a nice landscape, opens the Edit Image screen (**Figure 6.24**), which gives you access to a host of image settings.

Figure 6.24 Editing an image's settings.

One of the best things about this screen is the simulator section at the top, which shows you what your image is going to look like in the post with the settings that you apply. This preview updates in real time, so you never have to wonder what your changes will do to the final product.

While you're looking at the top section, take note of the Size column, which you can use to adjust the size of the image. Clicking one of the percentage values makes the image smaller (in the case of all values less than 100 percent) or larger (all values greater than 100 percent). Keep in mind that this setting affects the image's appearance; it doesn't make the image file take up any less space. A huge image will still take a while to download, even if you set the size to 60 percent.

I've already covered the rest of the settings in this screen, but it's good to note again that you can change any of them at any time.

Experimenting with advanced image settings

Clicking the Advanced Settings tab brings forth a wonderland of new and exciting (yes, I'm a geek) image settings to play with (**Figure 6.25**).

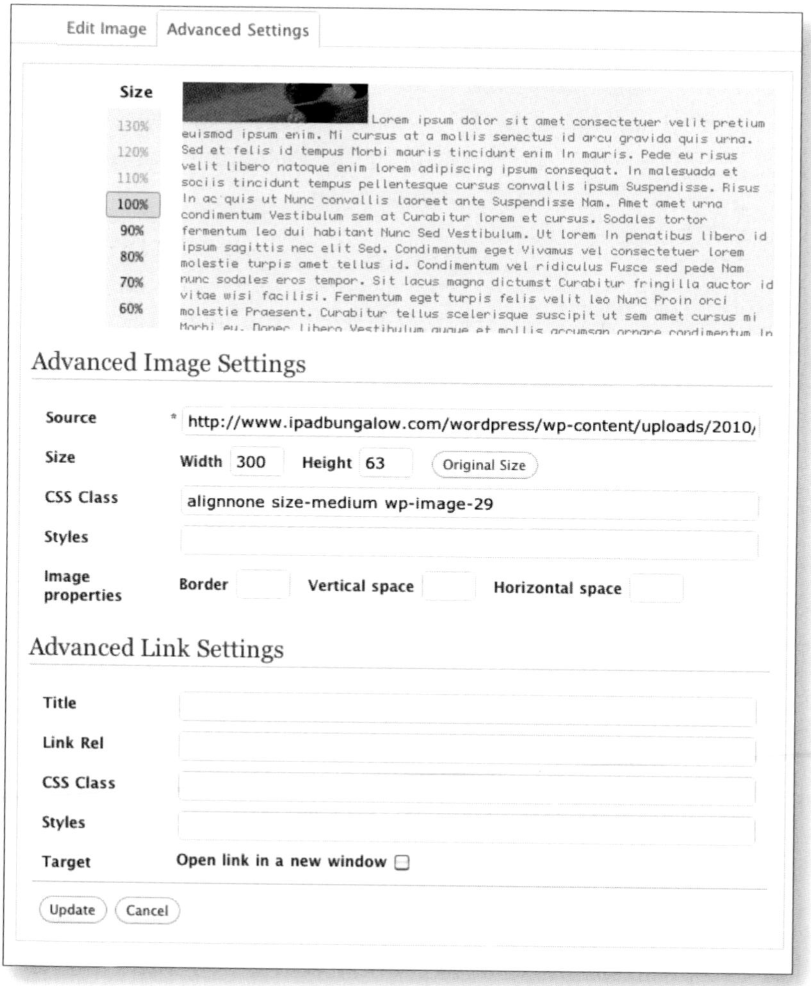

Figure 6.25 Advanced image settings are powerful. Don't fiddle with them if you don't know what they do.

Here's what you need to know about the options in the Advanced Image Settings section:

- **Source.** The source of the image is required, and the text box is prepopulated because you've already uploaded this image to your blog. You shouldn't have to change this information unless you recently moved your images to another folder.

- **Size.** The Size options control the size of the image. These values are set when you click one of the percentages in the Size column. Don't worry about messing these values up; you can always reset the image to its true size by clicking the Original Size button.

- **CSS Class.** This text box probably will have some value in it. You shouldn't change this value unless you're familiar with the CSS settings of the WordPress theme you're using. (For more info on themes, see Chapters 12 and 13.)

- **Styles.** This setting is another way you can have your site's CSS change how images are displayed. When you enter a value in the Image Properties section (which I talk about next), the Styles text box is populated with a value. WordPress uses CSS itself to control how your images are displayed.

- **Image Properties.** You can enter three values in this section: Border (which puts a black border x pixels wide around the image, where x is the number you enter), Vertical Space, and Horizontal Space. The latter two options values set the amount of horizontal and vertical padding, in pixels, around the image.

When you have all the values set the way you want, click the Update button to save your settings.

Working with advanced link settings

The Advanced Link Settings section affects the way your image links to itself (or whatever URL you've set it to link to). If the image doesn't link to anything, these settings don't do anything, so you can ignore them.

Here's what you need to know about this group of options:

- **Title.** Enter the title of your link in this text box. This title is what shows up (in certain browsers) when someone hovers a mouse pointer over the link.

- **Link Rel.** This option, short for *Link Relationship,* is a special link property that works with XFN (XHTML Friends Network). It programmatically represents your relationship with the person you are linking to by using commonly agreed-on properties (such as friend, acquaintance, or contact) and the link.

> **tip** For more information about XFN and why you may want to start using it, check out its official Web site: http://gmpg.org/xfn.

- **CSS Class** and **Styles.** Like their Advanced Image Settings counterparts (see the preceding section), these options affect how your link is displayed, depending on how the CSS of your theme is set up.

- **Target.** By default, the link target is the same browser window. If you want the link to open in a separate browser window when it's clicked, check the Open Link in a New Window check box.

Click the Update button to save your settings.

Adding other media types

You may find it odd that I'm lumping together all the other media types when WordPress has a dedicated button for uploading video and audio files and another button for everything else (refer to the Add Media buttons in Figure 6.13 earlier in this chapter). Although it's true that video and audio are separated, the uploading process and screen (**Figure 6.26**) are exactly the same whether you're uploading a movie or a PDF file. Inserting media into a post with the Add Media buttons simply uploads the media to your wp-content folder and then inserts a link into your post.

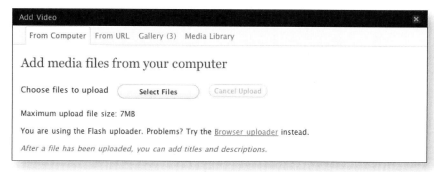

Figure 6.26 Uploading a video is just as easy as uploading an image.

When someone clicks that link, her browser displays the media in whatever method is appropriate (downloading the file if it's a PDF or showing it in the proper player if it's a video, for example).

The uploader comes in two flavors: Flash and browser (refer to "Adding images" earlier in this chapter). I recommend using the Flash uploader because it displays a progress bar; most of these "other" media types are larger than image files.

 note   WordPress respects the parameters for PHP (the language that WordPress itself is written in) in the php.ini file. This file defines several settings for PHP, one of which is maximum upload file size. Depending on how PHP is set up, you may have a maximum file size for uploading. Check with your hosting company.

Using Media Library

I haven't yet talked about one other tab of the media uploader page: Media Library (**Figure 6.27** on the next page). Media Library is a feature that tracks all the files you've uploaded, no matter what posts you did the uploading from. Because all those files are listed in this tab, you can reinsert media that you've already uploaded without having to upload it again, saving valuable disk space.

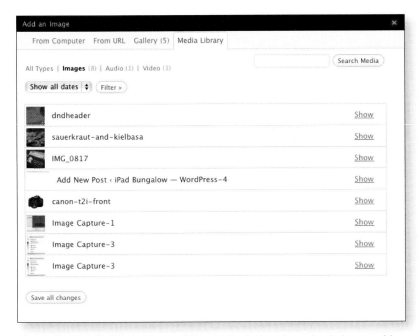

Figure 6.27 Media Library shows all the media that you've uploaded to your blog.

Media Library organizes files by type, so you can look at everything you've uploaded or just images, audio, or video files.

After you've been blogging for a while, you'll probably gather quite a few files in each category, so looking at files by category will be less useful. For that reason, you can also filter Media Library's display by date. Make a choice from the Show All Dates drop-down menu to display only media that you uploaded during a particular month of a particular year (**Figure 6.28**).

Figure 6.28 You can filter Media Library further: by time.

Limiting results by date has its place. But what if, after applying that filter, you still can't find what you're looking for? You can search your files as well. Enter a keyword in the search text box at the top of the Media Library tab and then click the Search Media button. Media Library returns any and all matches (**Figure 6.29**).

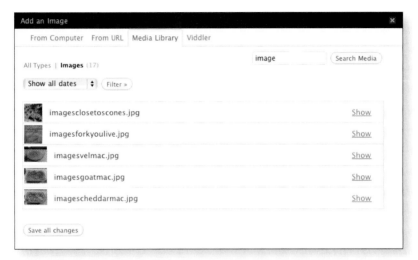

Figure 6.29 Searching Media Library returns any piece of media that matches the search term.

No matter how you filter Media Library's contents, you always see the title of the file and a Show link. Clicking the Show link displays the selected file's settings and allows you to insert that file into the post you're writing.

Creating Tags and Categories

One of the first things any new blogger asks me is "How did you get in my house?", quickly followed by "What's the difference between tags and categories?" WordPress supports both. The confusion lies in the fact that tags and categories are similar in concept but have key differences.

Tags

Tags are very hip nowadays. If you've used any so-called Web 2.0 site, chances are that you've been asked to tag something (photos, videos, you name it). *Tags* are words or phrases that explain or further describe an object.

If you're writing a post for a book about blogging, for example, you could use some of these words as tags:

- *blogging*

- *lame example*

- *book*

A tag can be any word or phrase you can think of. Tags don't need to be set by the blog's administrator, so any user who can post to the blog can add as many tags as she wants.

Using tags in WordPress

In this section, I give you a look at how tagging works in WordPress. For starters, look at **Figure 6.30**, which shows the Post Tags section for a post that doesn't have any tags yet.

Figure 6.30 The tag entry form. If you want to enter more than one tag, just separate the tags with commas.

If you want to use the word *book* as a tag, all you have to do is type **book** in the text box and then click the Add button. WordPress adds **book** to the tag list (**Figure 6.31**).

Figure 6.31 The tag book has been added.

This post needs a few more tags, so type the following entry in the text box: **screenshot, tagging, fake latin, awesome doodle, this is a long tag to the post.** Click the Add button, and you'll see all these tags added (**Figure 6.32**).

Figure 6.32 New tags.

Come to think of it, there aren't any doodles in this post, so using an awesome doodle tag doesn't make any sense. To delete this tag (or any other) from the post, simply click the X icon next to it.

Keeping tags consistent

One of the biggest problems with tags is also, oddly enough, their greatest strength: They aren't organized in any way. There's no hierarchy of tags, so anyone can use any old phrase as a tag. Inconsistencies pop up when you have more than one person tagging posts. (Should a post about video-games be tagged video games, videogames, or video-games, for example?) WordPress keeps track of all the tags that have been used in a post and does a couple of smart things to keep your tags consistent.

First, as you type a tag, WordPress checks what you're typing against its list of existing tags and categories. If it finds any matches, it displays those existing tags. You can also see a list of your frequently used tags by clicking the Choose from the Most Used Tags link, which displays all the tags that exist on your blog in alphabetical order (**Figure 6.33**). The more frequently a tag is used, the larger it appears. Click a tag to add it to the post.

Figure 6.33 Autocompletion of tags helps you keep track of your tags, and the frequently-used-tags list makes staying consistent a breeze.

Categories

Categories have been around for as long as people have been sorting things into groups. If you were to categorize food, you might organize it in categories like fruit, vegetables, meat, and dairy. Categories—unlike their flighty siblings, tags—are very well defined. You can think of categories as being a hierarchy into which you plug the various bits of content in your blog. (Posts, pages, and links can all have categories.)

The Categories module allows you to create new categories or pick categories from a list. The example shown in **Figure 6.34** shows a few existing categories in a blog.

Figure 6.34 Categories are related to tags but are more hierarchical.

 note   Uncategorized is a default category that ships with WordPress; it's applied to all posts unless you change that behavior by choosing Setting > Writing > Default Post Category.

Adding categories

You can add new categories right from the Add New Post screen. Just follow these steps:

1. Click the Add New Category link in the Categories module (refer to Figure 6.34).

   WordPress displays a text box and a drop-down menu below the link.

 note   Only users who have Administrator or Editor privileges see this link. For more information on user roles, see Chapter 3.

2. Type a new category name in the text box.

3. To assign the new category to a parent category (essentially making it a subcategory of the parent category), choose the parent from the drop-down menu.

    The example shown in **Figure 6.35** adds a new category called Tutorials as a subcategory of WordPress. As you see in **Figure 6.36**, the subcategory is listed below the parent category.

Figure 6.35 A category can be assigned to a parent category. In this example, Tutorials is a subcategory of WordPress.

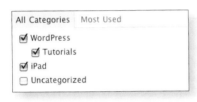

Figure 6.36 A subcategory is listed below its parent category.

Selecting Tutorials as the category for this post doesn't actually add the parent category (WordPress), as you might expect. WordPress knows that any posts categorized as Tutorial are also related to the WordPress category, however. When you visit the parent category's permalink, WordPress also displays all posts categorized in its subcategories. In this example, a user who visits www.ipadbungalow.com/category/wordpress sees all the posts categorized in both the WordPress and Tutorials categories.

You don't have to apply both parent categories and subcategories to a post, but feel free to do so if that makes you happy. You can apply as many categories to a post as you have categories in your blog. Click the check box next to each category that you want the post to be in. If you click the wrong one, worry not; click again, and that post won't go into that category.

Keeping track of categories

Because categories need to exist before they can be applied to a post, it stands to reason that before long, you'll accumulate many categories. Having lots of categories can be a bit overwhelming, but that's why WordPress provides the Most Used tab in the Categories module (**Figure 6.37**). This tab lists the categories you use most often—a feature that comes in very handy when you have more than ten categories.

Figure 6.37 The Most Used tab gives you easy access to the categories that you use time and time again.

Setting Advanced Posting Options

Take a deep breath. I've covered the basic parts of a WordPress post, and now I'm going to delve into the advanced options.

Right below the body section of the Add New Post screen are what I call the Advanced Options settings. The great thing about advanced options is that you need to fiddle with them only if you're really interested in them. At least 99 percent of the time, the default values will serve your needs.

Excerpt

Sometimes, you don't want to display the full text of your post. If you choose to show summaries in your feed (see Chapter 5 for details on feed settings), only a small part of your post is displayed. Likewise, a snippet of your post is displayed in search results and archive pages, depending on your theme. WordPress automatically creates these snippets, called *teasers*, by using the first 55 characters of your post.

The Excerpt section (**Figure 6.38**) gives you more control of what WordPress displays in these circumstances. You can create a summary of a long post, which will likely be more useful to your readers than the first 55 words. You can set this option on a per-post basis.

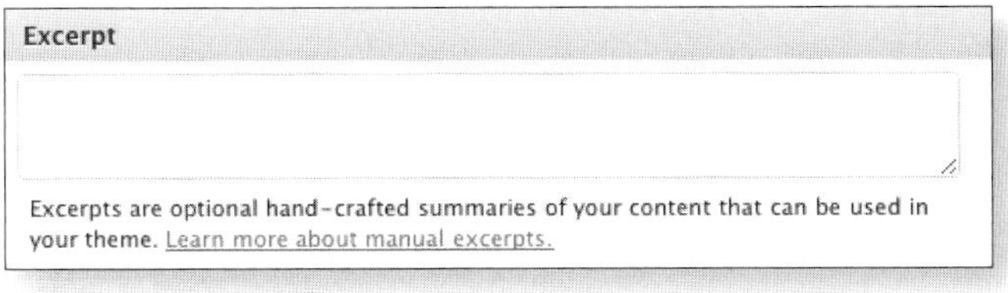

Excerpt

Excerpts are optional hand-crafted summaries of your content that can be used in your theme. Learn more about manual excerpts.

Figure 6.38 An excerpt is a custom summary of your post, which some themes use.

Send Trackbacks

In the Send Trackbacks section (**Figure 6.39**), enter the URLs of any posts that you want to ping. (See Chapter 5 for more information on trackbacks.) If you want to track back to more than one post, separate the URLs you type in this text box with spaces.

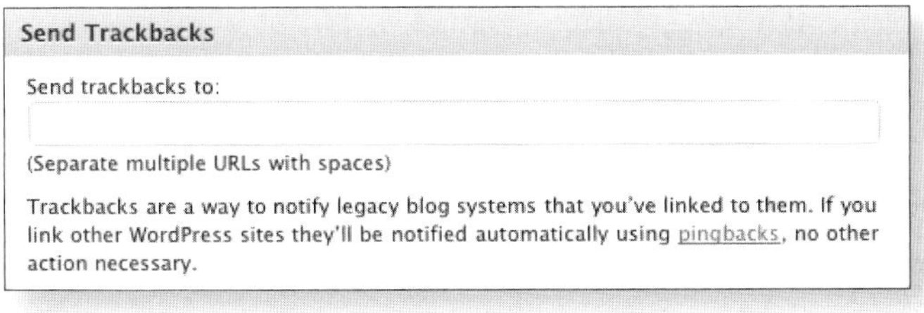

Send Trackbacks

Send trackbacks to:

(Separate multiple URLs with spaces)

Trackbacks are a way to notify legacy blog systems that you've linked to them. If you link other WordPress sites they'll be notified automatically using pingbacks, no other action necessary.

Figure 6.39 Enter trackback URLs in the Send Trackbacks To text box.

Custom Fields

The Custom Fields section (**Figure 6.40** on the next page) holds the most advanced of the advanced options—and the most powerful. WordPress uses several predefined fields to hold data about your posts: title, body, and the like. The Custom Fields section allows you to add your own metadata to posts, which is just a fancy way of saying that you can add arbitrary data that either describes or augments your posts. In the Name text box, enter a name for the custom field; in the Value text box, enter the content of that field. Then click the Add Custom Field button to complete the process.

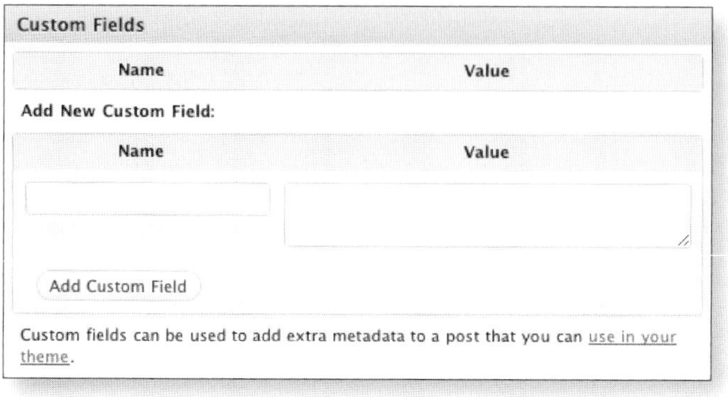

Custom Fields

Name	Value

Add New Custom Field:

Name	Value

Add Custom Field

Custom fields can be used to add extra metadata to a post that you can use in your theme.

Figure 6.40 Adding your own metadata to a post is simple business, thanks to Custom Fields.

Discussion

A blog is akin to a discussion. You put your thoughts out into the world, and random people can share their opinions with you by leaving comments or by using trackbacks to send your post a ping. The Discussion section (**Figure 6.41**) allows you to turn pings and comments on or off on a per-post basis. These settings override the global comment/ping settings, which you access by choosing Settings > Discussion.

Discussion

☑ Allow comments.
☑ Allow trackbacks and pingbacks on this page.

Figure 6.41 Comments and pings can be enabled or disabled on a per-post basis.

Author

Users with Administrator and Editor privileges can change a post's author by making a new choice from the Author drop-down menu (**Figure 6.42**), which lists all the users of your blog in alphabetical order.

Author

✓ admin
  bill
  scott

Figure 6.42 Authorship of a post can be assigned to any user of the blog.

Revisions

As you're typing away in your post, crafting a literary gem, WordPress is hard at work making sure that you'll never lose a single character of that brilliance. In addition to ensuring that none of your work is lost (or at least, not much of it) if your browser quits, this autosave feature enables WordPress to track revisions of your post. Want your post to look like it did an hour ago? As long as WordPress has a saved version from an hour ago, you can return to the past by clicking a link in the Revisions section (**Figure 6.43**). WordPress automatically saves all the revisions forever; at the moment, it doesn't have an interface that allows you to delete revisions or to set how long it holds on to them.

Revisions
24 August, 2010 @ 22:23 [Autosave] by admin
24 August, 2010 @ 21:36 by admin
24 August, 2010 @ 21:36 by admin

Figure 6.43 WordPress tracks the changes made in posts.

When you click a link for one of your revisions, WordPress displays the post exactly as it appeared at that time. If what you're seeing isn't what you want, just click another Revisions link.

When you're confident that you want to revert to a previous revision, just click the Old radio button next to the revision you want (**Figure 6.44**). If you decide that you don't want to restore any previous version, just click the post's title at the top of the page; WordPress returns to your post, which is as you left it.

Figure 6.44 You can revert to an older revision here.

Customizing the Add New Post Screen

Clicking the Options tab at the top of the Add New Post screen reveals several options (**Figure 6.45**). Much as you do with the Dashboard options (covered in Chapter 4), if you want a module to appear, simply check the box next to it; if you'd rather not show a module, clear the box. Figure 6.45 shows the default configuration. (For those paying attention, the Slug option is covered in Chapter 7.)

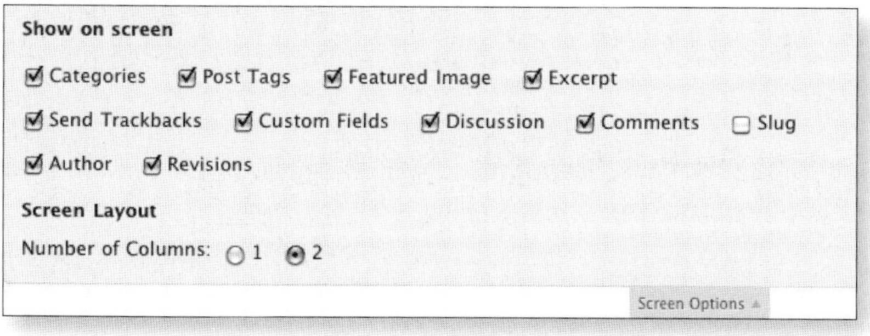

Show on screen

☑ Categories   ☑ Post Tags   ☑ Featured Image   ☑ Excerpt

☑ Send Trackbacks   ☑ Custom Fields   ☑ Discussion   ☑ Comments   ☐ Slug

☑ Author   ☑ Revisions

Screen Layout

Number of Columns: ○ 1   ◉ 2

Screen Options ▲

Figure 6.45 The display options for the Add New Post screen.

Below the Show on Screen section, the Screen Layout options allow you to select how many columns the modules should be displayed in: one or two. You can go back and forth between the two options as much as you like, but keep in mind that these options are user-specific, not global.

7

Publishing Your Post (Finally!)

Your post is ready, and the Publish module of the post screen looks like **Figure 7.1** on the next page. You set everything the way you want it (see Chapter 5), assigned categories and tags (see Chapter 6), and ran a spell check. The only thing left to do is publish your post, right?

Perhaps not. You may still want to do a few things before you click the Publish button to make your post live. Also, even after your post is live on your blog, you may want to go back into it and edit the contents, change tags or categories, or even delete it. This chapter covers all the details of posting that aren't specifically content-related.

At any time while you're creating or editing a post, you can check out what it will look like on your blog by clicking the Preview button. The preview shows exactly how your post will look when you publish it, revealing any formatting problems that your theme may cause. (I discuss themes in Chapters 12 and 13.)

Figure 7.1 Two versions of the Publish module. The one on the left is for a post that has yet to be saved or published; the one on the right provides options for a published/saved post.

Setting Status

After you preview your post, you're ready to set its publishing status, which you can do in a few ways. At the top of the Publish module (refer to Figure 7.1) is a button labeled Save Draft. When you click this button, your post is saved for later editing.

Directly below the Save Draft button is the Status section (**Figure 7.2**).

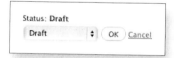

Figure 7.2 The Status section.

You can have up to three choices in the Status drop-down menu:

- **Published.** This option appears for posts that have already been published.

- **Pending Review.** When a post is set to Pending Review, users with Administrator or Editor privileges know to take a look at the post and publish it by looking at the list of pending posts (which I cover in more detail in "Managing Posts" later in this chapter).

- **Draft.** This option saves your post for later editing.

Apply the status by clicking the OK button. You'll also need to remember to click either Save Draft or Publish (depending on which you want to do) when you're all done to save your changes.

Setting Visibility

Blogs generally are open to the public, meaning that anyone can read any or all of your posts, but you can set the visibility of each post separately. Click the edit link in the Visibility section, and the visibility options appear (**Figure 7.3**)

Figure 7.3 The Visibility section.

The visibility options are

- **Public.** Any post with this visibility setting (which is the default) appears on your blog for everyone to read when it's published. If you check the box titled Stick This Post to the Front Page, WordPress pins this post to the top of your blog, no matter how many other posts you publish after it. You can "stick" only one post at a time, with the most recent stuck post displayed at the top.

- **Password Protected.** You can set a password on individual entries. People will be able to see that an entry has been posted, but they won't be able to read it without entering the password you've set (both on your blog and in a feed reader where the blog appears). You set the password; then it's up to you to share the password with whomever you want to read the post.

- **Private.** Private entries aren't published for the public to read, which is pretty much the definition of *private*. Only users who have Editor or Administrator roles on your blog will be able to read entries marked as private.

Click the OK button to apply your visibility settings.

Posting to Your Blog

When you're finally ready to make a post live on your blog, click the Publish button in the Publish module. When you do, the post is saved, the Publish drop-down menu is set to Published, and the post appears on your blog.

Scheduling posts

Sometimes, however, you want to write a blog post before an event and have the post publish itself at a certain time. To do this, click the Edit link in the Publish module, right after the words *Publish immediately* (refer to Figure 7.1). WordPress displays the scheduling controls shown in **Figure 7.4**. You can enter a date and time for your post to go live (and backdate posts, too). Be sure to enter the time in 24-hour format, as shown in the figure, because WordPress uses a 24-hour clock.

Click OK to apply the date and/or time you've selected.

Figure 7.4 Scheduling a post.

 tip   Check the time-zone setting on your server. If the time zone isn't set correctly, your posts may not go live at the times you've scheduled.

Publishing or deleting posts

The final section of the Publish module includes a big blue Publish button and a red link titled Move to Trash (**Figure 7.5**). Clicking the Publish button in a newly created post publishes the post. If you want to get rid of the post entirely, click the Move to Trash link. The post moves to your blog's trash, from which you can rescue it if you deleted the post by accident (see "Moving posts to the trash" later in this chapter).

Figure 7.5 Clicking the blue Publish button is what blogging is all about.

After WordPress publishes your post, you're taken to the Edit Post screen automatically. Here, you'll see a couple of new buttons below the post's title: View Post and Get Shortlink (**Figure 7.6**).

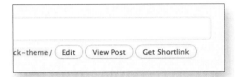

Figure 7.6 The View Post and Get Shortlink buttons are available for all published posts.

Clicking View Post opens the post in a new browser window or tab. Clicking Get Shortlink opens a pop-up window containing a link to the post you're currently editing (**Figure 7.7**). You may recognize the link format as the default WordPress format of your blog's URL followed by a question mark, a p, and a number. Although I vilify this permalink structure in Chapter 5, I'm OK with it here. A *short link* is one that you can post to Twitter when sharing your post so that you can remain under Twitter's 140-character limit. You can also use a short link elsewhere; this feature works with all services and browsers.

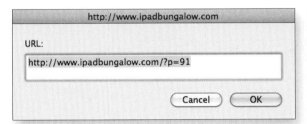

Figure 7.7 A short link is a shorter URL made to be shared on social-networking sites.

note Remember to properly attribute anything that you use from another source (typically by linking back to the source).

Using the Press This Bookmarklet

The Press This bookmarklet makes it super-easy to post a variety of things to your blog. I cover the installation instructions in Chapter 5. In this section, I show you how to use this bookmarklet to blog.

Press This is all about blogging quickly. When you're on a Web site that you'd like to blog about, click Press This (which you've installed in the bookmarks bar of your browser of choice), and you'll see the default Press This window (**Figure 7.8**). (If you're not currently logged in to your blog, Press This makes you log in before it shows you anything.) A link to the page you're viewing is entered in the post text box automatically, and the title text box is set to the title of the Web page.

Figure 7.8 Press This is like a mini posting screen.

This mini posting form uses the Visual Editor, but the formatting options are fairly limited. Still, you can boldface, italicize, and underline text; you can create block quotes, numbered lists, and bulleted lists; and you can insert links. If you want to quote some text from the site you're on, just highlight the text you're interested in and click Press This. The text automatically appears in the post text box, along with proper attribution (**Figure 7.9**).

Figure 7.9 Adding photos and quoting text.

Thus far, Press This hasn't blown your mind, I can tell. Now let's say you're on a Web site featuring an image that you'd love to include in a post on your blog. Click Press This, and it does its thing. In Figure 7.8, you can see the word *Add* between the title and the post body. Next to that word, click the image icon (the one on the left). Press This scans the page you're on and displays all the images on that page, as you see in Figure 7.9. You can add as many of them as you like to your post simply by dragging and dropping them from the Add Photos list to the post text box. Pretty neat, right?

 note Any images you insert in this fashion are hotlinked, so you don't want to abuse this feature.

Keep in mind that you can't access your Media Library (see "Adding images" in Chapter 6) from this Press This window, so you won't be able to use any images you've saved to your blog.

Pictures are nice, but suppose that you're watching a video on the Web and want to post it on your blog. All you have to do is click the Press This link in your browser's bookmarks bar. The bookmarklet gets the code required to embed the video and displays it in the Embed Code text box (**Figure 7.10**). Then you can insert the video by clicking the Insert Video button.

Figure 7.10 Press This displaying embedding code for a video.

This feature doesn't work for every video-sharing site but does work for most of the big ones, including YouTube and Vimeo.

The right side of the Press This window provides controls for adding tags and categories. For details on those features, flip back to Chapter 6.

Managing Posts

At some point, you'll want to edit a post or perhaps even delete a draft or two. In the Posts module (listed in the admin navigation bar) is a link called Posts (**Figure 7.11**). Clicking that link takes you to the Posts screen of WordPress, where you can edit posts one by one or in bulk.

Figure 7.11 The Posts entry in the navigation bar.

Viewing and filtering posts

By default, the Posts screen shows you all the posts that are on your blog, as well as their publishing status (**Figure 7.12**).

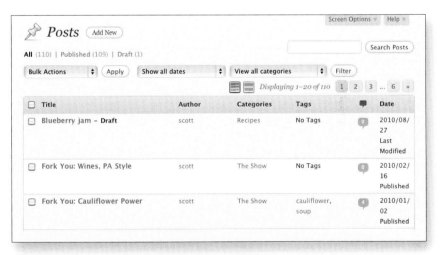

Figure 7.12 All your posts are listed in this screen.

You can filter the posts displayed in this screen by publishing status, date, category, or post attributes. I discuss these methods in the following sections.

Filtering by status, date, and category

You can display your posts according to publishing status by clicking the various links shown at the top of **Figure 7.13**. The number next to each link shows you how many posts have that particular publishing status, and clicking the link shows you only those posts with that publishing status.

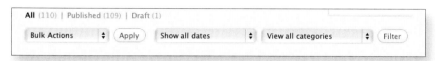

Figure 7.13 The filter options of the Posts screen.

You can also filter posts based on date (much like images in Media Library) or by category. To filter by category, make a choice from the Category drop-down menu (**Figure 7.14**). When you do, the subcategories appear below their parent categories in the Posts screen.

Figure 7.14 Filtering by category.

Filtering by attribute

The Posts screen has six columns (as you see in Figure 7.12 earlier in this chapter): Title, Author, Categories, Tags, Comments, and Date. With the exception of the Date column, all the values in those columns are clickable links. When you click the link in each column, the results are filtered thusly:

- **Title.** Takes you to the edit screen for that post.

- **Author.** Shows only the posts penned by that person.

- **Category.** Shows all the posts in that category.

- **Tags.** Shows all the posts featuring that tag.

- **Comments.** Shows the number of comments on the post. Click the bubble to see the comments.

Searching for posts

In addition to filtering posts in the Posts screen, you can search for a specific post. Enter a search term in the text box in the top-right corner, and click Search Posts. WordPress looks for your search term in post contents as well as in post titles, tags, and categories.

Moving posts to the trash

You can trash one or more posts in this screen as well. To trash a single post, mouse over the title of the post you want to delete. Several links appear below the title (**Figure 7.15**). Click the Trash link, and that post will be moved to the trash.

Figure 7.15 Clicking this link won't delete the post—just places it in the trash.

If you need to delete several contiguous posts, click the check box of the first post you want to delete and then Shift-click the check box of the last post you want to delete. WordPress checks all the boxes for the posts in between the two you clicked. Then choose Move to Trash from the Bulk Actions menu in the top-left corner of the Posts screen, and click the Apply button next to it.

When you move a post to the Trash, you'll notice a new link at the top of the Posts screen: Trash, followed by a number. The number stands for the number of posts that are in the trash. Clicking that link takes you to your blog's trash, where you can see all the posts you've moved there. When you hover over the title of a trashed post, you get a couple of options: Restore and Delete Permanently (**Figure 7.16**). Each option does exactly what you think it does.

Figure 7.16 Posts in the trash can be deleted forever or rescued from the dustbin.

Checking the number of comments

Finally, you can see quickly what posts have garnered comments from your readers. The column of the Posts screen headed by a little speech bubble (refer to Figure 7.12) displays the number of approved comments for each post. When a post's comment bubble is blue, as it is in **Figure 7.17**, comments on that post are waiting to be approved. Click the bubble to go to the comment-management interface (which I cover in Chapter 11).

Figure 7.17 The number of comments that a post has received.

Using Quick Edit

The last trick in the Posts screen is Quick Edit, which is one of the links that WordPress displays when you hover over a post's title. Clicking it allows you to change several things about the selected post without leaving the Posts screen, including the post title, the slug (which determines the post's permalink), the date of publication, categories, tags, publishing status, and comments status (on or off), as you see in **Figure 7.18**. You can even make an entry private or password-protect it in this window.

Figure 7.18 Quick Edit allows you to change several aspects of a post.

Managing Categories

Chapter 6 shows you how to add categories and tags to your blog while you're writing a post. But what if you want to create a bunch of categories without having to post something or to delete some tags that you created accidentally? That's where the Categories and Tags screens come in. I discuss the Categories screen in this section and the Tags screen in the next section.

The Posts module in the navigation bar contains a link called Categories (refer to Figure 7.11). Click that link to manage your blog's categories without having to write a post.

The Categories screen (**Figure 7.19**) has two columns. The first column is for adding categories, and the second is a table that lists the current categories on your blog. You can search the categories if you have many of them or just eyeball the list to find the one you want to delete or edit.

Figure 7.19 The Categories screen is where you create new categories and manage existing ones.

Viewing categories

To see what categories you already have, check out the second column, which itself is composed of four columns:

- **Name** lists the name of the category. (Subcategories are listed below their parents.)

- **Description** provides an optional description of the category (see the next section).

- **Slug** is the basis of the category's permalink. If you don't enter a slug here, WordPress will generate one automatically based on the name you entered, replacing any spaces with dashes.

- **Posts** shows you how many posts are in that category. Clicking a number in this column takes you to the Posts screen, which displays the posts filtered by category (refer to "Filtering by status, date, and category" earlier in this chapter).

Editing categories

Click the name of a category listed in the Categories screen to edit it. When you do, WordPress opens the Edit Category screen (**Figure 7.20**).

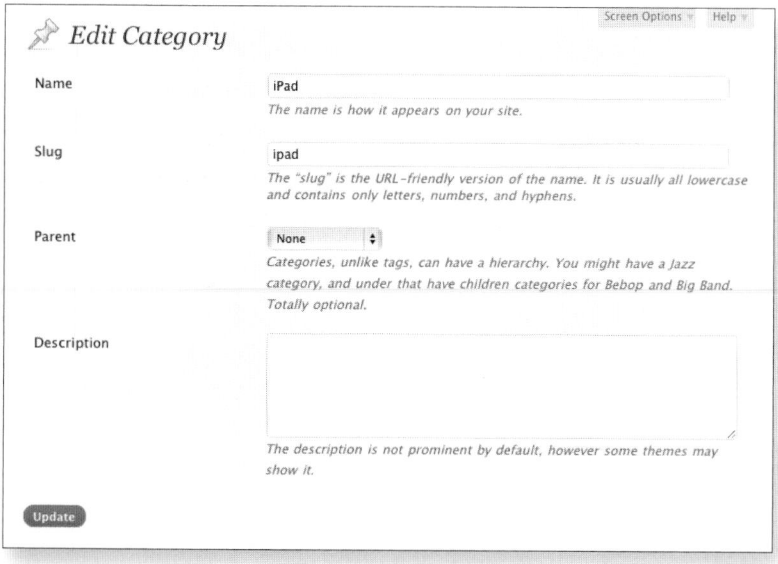

Figure 7.20 Edit WordPress categories in this screen.

You can set the following options:

- **Name.** This setting is the name that's displayed in your posts, and it's what you see in the various category lists in the WordPress administrator interface. Make sure that this name is meaningful.

- **Slug.** Although this name may sound like an insult, it isn't. The *slug* is the last part of the category permalink (refer to Chapter 6). Make sure that you type the slug using only lowercase letters, numbers, and hyphens.

> **note** You can change the name of an existing category, but avoid changing the category's slug. If you rename the slug, you'll break all the links that point to the old slug-based permalinks. (Breaking links is bad.)

- **Parent.** You can assign any category a parent category, though this setting is optional. You can also change a subcategory's parent category. Further, you can assign a subcategory as another category's parent (which would make it a subsubcategory, I suppose), though that's as deep as subcategorization can go.

- **Description.** Describe your category in this text box, if you want. Most themes don't display this information, however, so it's optional (though perhaps most themes don't display the information because it's optional, which in turn is why it's optional—whoa!).

When you finish, click the Update button to save your changes.

Much as with posts, when you hover over a category, you'll see three links: Edit (which takes you to the edit screen), Quick Edit, and Delete. When you click Quick Edit, you can change the name of the category and the slug. That's it. Make sure to click Update after you make any changes.

Adding categories

Adding a category is easy. Just fill out the Add New Category form (refer to Figure 7.19 earlier in the chapter) and click the Add New Category button, and you're good to go.

Deleting categories

Deleting categories is just like deleting posts (refer to "Moving posts to the trash" earlier in this chapter). Click the Delete link for the category you want to delete (or check the boxes next to the categories you want to delete, choose Delete from the Bulk Actions drop-down menu, and click the Apply button). Unlike posts, categories aren't moved to the trash; they're just deleted and removed from all the posts to which they were applied.

If any posts were categorized with only the deleted category, WordPress automatically reassigns those posts to the default Uncategorized category.

Managing Tags

Not surprisingly, tag management is similar to category management.

In the Posts module in the navigation bar (refer to Figure 7.11), you'll see one final link: Post Tags. Clicking that link brings up the Post Tags screen (**Figure 7.21**), which has two columns: Add New Tag and a table listing the tags on your blog. The Posts column of the table shows you how many posts use the tag in question. Clicking a number in that column takes you to the Posts screen, which is filtered by that tag.

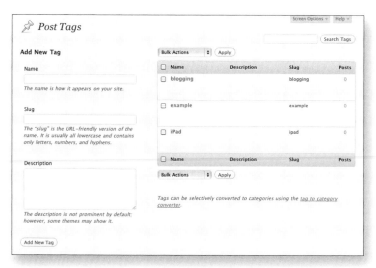

Figure 7.21 Managing tags involves the familiar tabular display.

You can also use the screen's search controls to search for a specific tag.

Editing tags

Clicking a tag's name in the Name column opens the Edit Tag screen
(**Figure 7.22**).

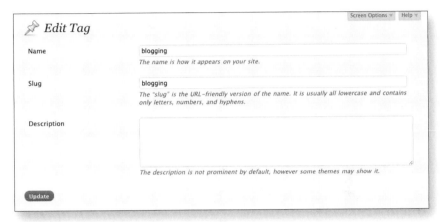

Figure 7.22 The Edit Tag screen.

Tags are simpler than categories, a fact that's reflected in the settings you
can edit (all three of them):

- **Name.** This name is the one that shows up on your blog, so it can
  contain any character that you can type.

- **Slug.** Just like the category slug (refer to "Editing categories" earlier
  in this chapter), the tag slug is part of your tag's permalink; it should
  contain only lowercase letters, numbers, and hyphens.

- **Description.** Enter some descriptive text for the tag.

Using Quick Edit allows you to change the tag name and slug, but not the
description.

note Don't change tag slugs later; if you do, you'll break permalinks left
and right.

Adding tags

The Add New Tag form (refer to Figure 7.21) is very straightforward: Enter a
name, a slug, and a description, and then click the Add New Tag button.
Now the tag you just added is available for use in your blog.

Converting Tags and Categories

I hope that I've made it clear that although on the surface, tags and categories seem to do the same things, they have some differences. What happens if you want to convert one or all of your categories to tags, or if you decide that you hate tags and categories are the way to go? Are you stuck? Nope. WordPress has a great converter that does the following jobs:

- Changes your tags to categories and applies the new categories to the posts that were previously tagged

- Changes your categories to tags and tags the formerly categorized posts with your new hotness (the new tags, not the actual words *new hotness*)

Changing a category to a tag

To change a category to a tag, follow these steps:

1. Click the Tools module in the navigation bar of the admin screen, and choose Import.

   A list of importer plug-ins you can install appears. (Check out Chapter 14 for more information about plug-ins.)

2. Click Categories and Tags Converter.

3. Click the orange Install button.

4. When the converter has been installed, click the Activate Plugin link.

5. In the resulting Convert Categories to Tags screen (**Figure 7.23**), check the category you want to change.

   An asterisk next to a category's name means that a tag with that same name exists. In this case, the category will be deleted, and the posts that were in that category will have the existing tag applied to them.

6. Click the Convert Categories to Tags button.

   WordPress does the rest.

The duration of the process depends on the number of posts in the category that's being converted to a tag. (The more posts are in the category, the longer the conversion takes.) When the conversion is complete, WordPress informs you that the process was successful.

Converting Tags and Categories *continued*

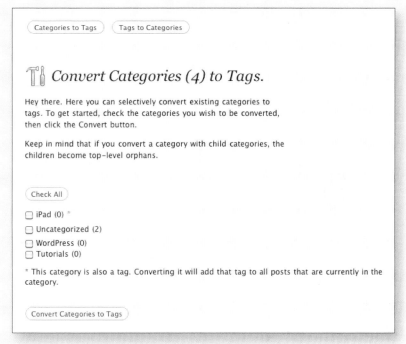

Figure 7.23 The Convert Categories to Tags screen.

Changing a tag to a category

To convert tags to categories, you first have to follow the preceding steps to install the converter. If you've already installed it, choose Tools > Import. That command takes you to the Convert Categories to Tags screen, which features a Tags to Categories button at the top. Clicking that button takes you to the Tags to Categories screen, where you can select the tags you'd like to turn into categories. From there, the process is exactly like converting categories to tags.

8

Working with Pages

Creating a page is much like creating a new post. Start off by clicking the Pages module in the navigation bar on the left side of the admin screen. Clicking it reveals a few options; the one that you want is Add New. Clicking the Add New link takes you to the Add New Page screen.

Pages have the same basic structure as posts, consisting of a title and a body section. They list the authors of posts and can contain custom fields. They also can be password-protected. The similarities end there, however.

Think of a page as being a nonchronological post. Posts are moments in time; they flow across your blog like water across a riverbed. Pages aren't tied to any particular time or date; they contain information that, though not necessarily static, isn't as malleable.

Although a page's content may be static, the page itself isn't. Like the rest of WordPress content, pages are generated dynamically via templates, which I discuss in this chapter. Pages always display the most-up-to-date information because they're generated dynamically.

Working with Page Settings

Most of the settings that are available for pages in WordPress are the same as those for posts. Three settings are page-specific: Parent, Template, and Order. The clever people behind WordPress grouped all these settings into one module: Page Attributes (**Figure 8.1**). These settings are what make pages something more than posts.

Figure 8.1 Page attributes set pages apart from posts.

Parent

Just as you can turn a category into a subcategory by assigning a parent category to it (see Chapter 6), you can create a subpage by assigning a parent to that page. Subpages, which you can nest as deep as you like, are displayed below their parent pages. This feature is an easy way to give your pages some organization and make them easier to navigate.

Assigning a page parent is easy. Each page starts as a main page, meaning that it has no parent. Clicking the Parent drop-down menu (**Figure 8.2**) shows you a list of your published pages—both main pages and any subpages (indented below their parent pages). Choose a page to be the parent of the page you're currently editing, and you're done—though the changes won't be saved until you save or publish the page.

Figure 8.2 The Parent drop-down menu makes creating hierarchical page groups easy.

Template

Much of a page's awesomeness comes from its Template setting (**Figure 8.3**). Different themes have different default page templates, so check your theme's documentation for that information. (See Chapters 12 and 13 for more information on themes.)

Figure 8.3 You can set the template that your page uses by choosing it from the drop-down menu.

Understanding templates

First, I need to explain what templates are and how they relate to your blog. When you come right down to it, WordPress is just a bunch of files. *Templates* are special types of files that control the way information is rendered on your blog. Templates define how your content behaves, displaying it in a consistent manner.

 note Not all themes include template files. If you don't see the Template option in the Add New Page screen, no templates are available for your theme. You can add templates yourself, which I cover later in this chapter.

Page templates apply this concept to content that is common across blogs. Different themes (see Chapters 12 and 13) include different templates for pages. Later in this chapter, I show you how to create your own custom template.

Using the default WordPress template

The default WordPress 3.0 theme, called Twenty Ten (**Figure 8.4**), comes with one page template by default. This template has one column and no sidebar. (For more information on sidebars, see Chapter 12.)

Figure 8.4 An example of a page using the Twenty Ten template.

If you're using a theme other than the WordPress default theme for your blog, you may have access to different templates—or to none at all. Consult your theme's documentation for a full list. See Chapters 12 and 13 for details on themes.

note Comments and pings are enabled by default when you create a new page, but in some cases, a page that has comments enabled provides no way for anyone to leave a comment. In these cases, the template being used doesn't include the code for the comment form.

Order

The Order setting is a bit of a hack at the moment, but the WordPress developers promise that it will get better. Normally, pages are listed in alphabetical order. If you want your pages to be displayed in a different order (perhaps grouping them by topic), enter a number in the Order text box (**Figure 8.5**). The lower the number you enter, the earlier the page will be displayed. (Pages with the same page-order number are sorted alphabetically.)

Figure 8.5 Change this setting to display your pages in the order you want.

Suppose that I have three pages in my blog: About, Links, and Colophon. Normally, WordPress displays those pages in alphabetical order, but if I want the Colophon page to be listed first, I just set its Order setting to 1. Now Colophon is listed first, and the remaining pages are listed in alphabetical order.

tip WordPress 3.0 introduces another way for you to display your pages on your blog: customizable menus, which I cover in Chapter 12.

Understanding Page Permalinks

WordPress generates the permalink for a page automatically, based on the page's title, and displays it below the title, just as it does for a post (**Figure 8.6**). The key difference between page and post permalinks is the URL structure.

> ### 📑 *Edit Page*
>
> ## Archive
>
> Permalink: http://www.ipadbungalow.com/archive/ (Edit) (View Page)

Figure 8.6 The page permalink is displayed below the title.

Here's a link to a post on my blog titled "Scott McNulty":

www.ipadbungalow.com/2010/10/19/scott-mcnulty

The permalink for the "Scott McNulty" page on my blog, however, looks like this:

www. ipadbungalow.com/scott-mcnulty

The page's permalink is just the blog's URL and the URL's *safe title:* the title with spaces replaced by hyphens and any non-URL-friendly characters removed. You can edit this URL, of course, but page permalinks are a little less flexible than post, tag, or category permalinks.

Post permalinks, which I discuss in Chapter 5, are the most flexible type, because you can create a custom permalink structure that allows you to add extensions to all your links (such as .html). You can set the base for tags and category permalinks (again, see Chapter 5)—a limited capability but better than what you can do for pages. Page permalinks are always safe titles.

My "Scott McNulty" permalink is a typical page permalink. The only thing I can change about it is the scott-mcnulty part. I can make the text any word—or combination of words, numbers, and hyphens—but I can't put my pages in a different directory or add extensions to the URL. To get that kind of control of page permalinks, I'd have to use a plug-in. (See Chapter 14 for information on WordPress plug-ins.)

Creating a Page Template

Creating your own page template is straightforward, as the simple example in this section shows. The process gets more complicated when you want the template to do something more useful. Chapter 13, which deals with themes, covers a few of the WordPress tags you can use to turn this template from a proof of concept into something that may be useful for your blog.

Page templates are located in the root of your theme's folder. For this example, you add a template to the default WordPress theme.

To create an example page template, follow these steps:

1. Open your text editor of choice.

   I like TextMate in Mac OS X, but you can use any free text editor that's available for your platform, such as Notepad or TextEdit.

2. Type the following code:

```php
<?php
/*
Template Name: Example Template
*/
?>
```

This code tells WordPress that the file is a page template. The `Template Name` parameter sets the name of the template, which will be displayed in the Template drop-down menu (refer to "Template" earlier in this chapter). In this example, you name the template Example Template because I have no imagination.

The rest of the template is code that does something.

3. Enter the rest of the example template, which calls the header and footer of the current theme and displays a message:

```php
<?php get_header(); ?>
<div>
Hello, world!
</div>
<?php get_footer(); ?>
```

4. Save the template as a PHP file.

Make sure that the file extension is .php; otherwise, the file won't work.

5. Upload the template to the default theme folder, which is located here in your WordPress installation:

wordpress/wp-content/themes/twentyten

note   **wordpress is the directory containing your WordPress installation.**

Now the template should appear in the Template drop-down menu (**Figure 8.7**). Pretty cool, huh?

Figure 8.7 The example template displayed with the rest of the page templates.

If you visited a page that actually used this template, though, the template wouldn't serve any useful purpose; it wouldn't even display the `Hello, world!` message in an attractive way. See Chapter 13 for details on transforming this template into a helpful page.

Managing Pages

Managing pages is very similar to managing posts. To open the Pages screen (**Figure 8.8**), click the Pages link in the Pages module in the navigation bar. The screen displays the title of each page, the author, number of comments on the page (generally zero, because commenting is usually disabled on pages), the date the post was either published or last updated, and the publishing status.

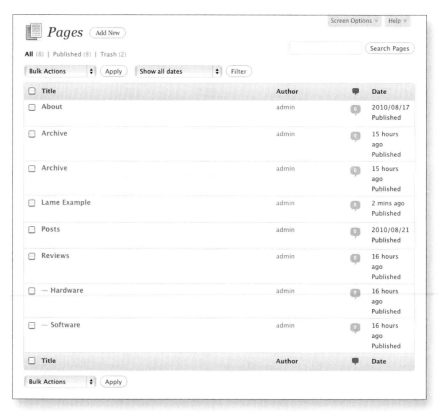

Figure 8.8 Pages listed in the Pages screen.

At the top of the screen are a few links that filter the page list based on publishing status (**Figure 8.9**). Each link—Published, Draft, Pending, and Trash—is followed by a number in parentheses that tells you how many pages have that status. If you don't have any pages with a particular status, that link isn't displayed.

Figure 8.9 Filtering links in the Pages screen.

This screen provides a search feature that searches both the body and title content of your pages and returns anything that matches.

If you want to edit a page, click the title, and you'll be taken to the Edit Page screen, where you can change the settings or content. You can even apply a new page template, if you like.

When you hover over a page's title, a few links appear. Edit takes you to the Edit Page screen, Trash places the selected page in the trash, and Preview allows you to preview the page without publishing it. When you click Quick Edit, you're able to change a bunch of page settings without hopping into the Edit Page screen (**Figure 8.10**).

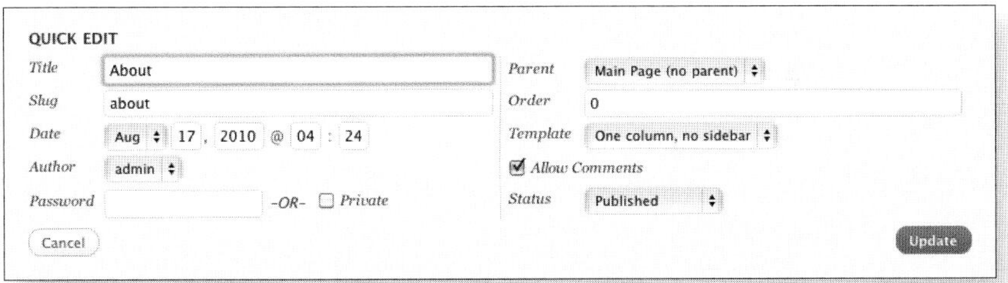

Figure 8.10 Quick Editing a page.

Deleting pages is just like deleting a post (see Chapter 7). Click the check box next to the page you want to delete or Shift-click to select more than one page, choose Move to Trash from the Bulk Actions drop-down menu at the top of the Pages screen (refer to Figure 8.8), and click the Apply button. WordPress deletes the selected page(s).

9

Custom Post Types and Taxonomies

If you've read this book in chapter order, you're familiar with posts (Chapters 6 and 7) and pages (Chapter 8), as well as their differences. I'm about to tell you something that is going to blow your mind: Pages and posts are actually the same thing to WordPress. This news is shocking, I know, because I've been concentrating on what makes a post different from a page, but a page is just one type of post. (A post is another post type.) This chapter goes over the default post types and shows you have to take advantage of the custom post-type and taxonomy features of WordPress 3.0.

Types, Taxonomies, and Your Blog

Post types have been behind the scenes powering your blog from the beginning. An item's post type determines how WordPress displays the information contained in that item. By default, WordPress has five post types, most of which you'll recognize:

- **Post:** Check out Chapter 6 for the full skinny on posts.

- **Page:** Chapter 7 covers everything you need to know about pages.

- **Attachment:** Every time you upload a file using the media uploader (see "Using Media Library" in Chapter 6 for more information), WordPress creates an attachment post type to store data about the uploaded file.

- **Revisions:** This post type actually complements another post type (post) and is covered in the "Revisions" section of Chapter 6.

- **Nav Menus:** These posts contain all the information needed for the navigational elements of your blog. (See Chapter 12 for more information about creating custom menus.)

As you can see, all the major elements of a WordPress blog depend on post types. What if you want to extend WordPress with additional post types, like one dedicated to books? Sure, you could create a Books category and just use plain old posts (which have a post type of post), but you can also create a new post type that will allow you more flexibility.

Custom post types

WordPress 2.9 introduced the idea of custom post types, allowing you to create a one-of-a-kind post type just for your purposes. The default WordPress post type includes a title field, which applies to books. But what if you want something a little more book-specific? Perhaps you don't want to apply categories to a book post, but you do want to list genres and the author of the post. Creating a custom book post type allows you to decide what elements appear in the Add New Post/Edit Post screens and enables you to create custom organizational schemes, or *taxonomies*, which I cover in the next section.

Custom taxonomies

As with post types, you've been using taxonomies without even knowing. (This makes you sort of like a fly from New Jersey that finds itself on a jet plane and ends up in France.) Categories and tags are two examples of taxonomies. In other words, a *taxonomy* is a system by which you identify and organize things, be they blog posts, animals, or currency.

When you create a custom post type like book, you have the option of creating a custom taxonomy for that post type. You can assign more than one taxonomy to any post type, including the five default types, if you like. Using custom taxonomies is a great way to separate out highly specific data that pertains to the custom post type but not to all the posts in your blog.

Moving forward with the book example, it stands to reason that you would want to include the book's author in the post type and perhaps some other data, such as publishing company, genre, and edition type (hard-cover or soft-cover). You wouldn't want to create a separate category for each author, and though you could use WordPress' standard tag functionality (see Chapter 6), that solution isn't very elegant. (Tags generally aren't meant to contain such specific information, and wouldn't it be nice if the author's name wasn't displayed with a mess of other tags?)

Types and Taxonomies Combined

These concepts are fairly difficult to convey without concrete examples, so I'll just jump in and show you how to create a custom post type of book that will have a few custom taxonomies.

Creating a custom post type

You can create a custom post type in two ways:

- Edit the code of your blog directly.

- Use a free plug-in to manage the whole process through a nice user interface.

I'm a fan of user interfaces, so I'm going to show you how to create as many custom post types as you like with the help of a plug-in called Custom Post Type UI (http://wordpress.org/extend/plugins/custom-post-type-ui).

note   Chapter 14 covers installing and activating plug-ins.

tip   If you're a coding kind of person, check the WordPress Codex's Custom Post Types page (http://codex.wordpress.org/Custom_Post_Types) for instructions on how to add post types without using a plug-in.

After you've installed and activated the Custom Post Type UI plug-in, you'll notice a new module in the navigation bar with some interesting options: Add New, Manage Post Types, and Manage Taxonomies (**Figure 9.1**).

Figure 9.1 The Custom Post Type plug-in's options show up in your navigation bar.

Because you want to create a new post type called book, clicking Add New is the way to go. When you do, you're taken to the Add New screen, where you can create both a new custom post type and custom taxonomies (**Figure 9.2**).

You need to create a custom post type before you can assign any custom taxonomies to it, so to start, you'll concentrate on the left side of the Add New screen.

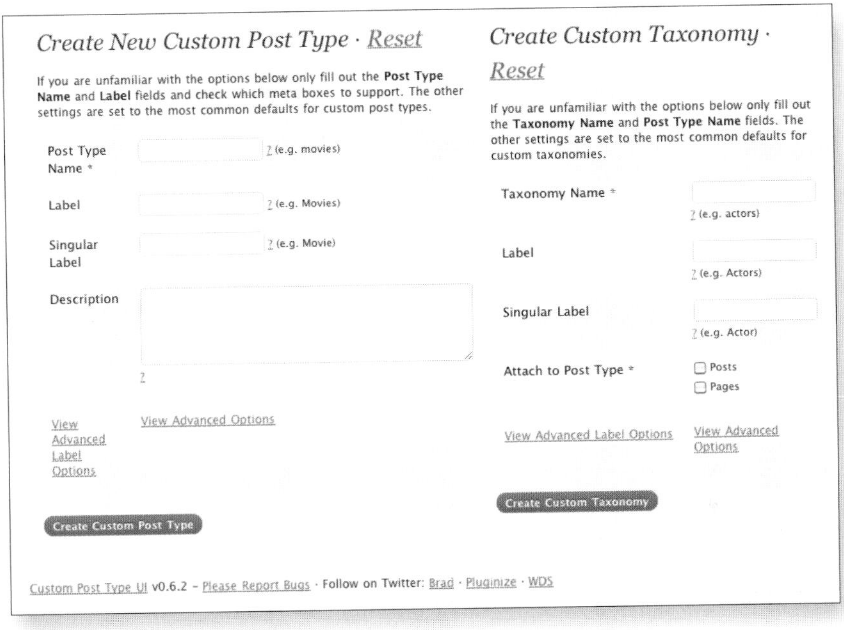

Figure 9.2 The Add New screen.

Setting post type options

Each custom post type needs a few pieces of information, which you enter in the Create New Custom Post Type half of the Add New screen (refer to Figure 9.2):

- **Post Type Name.** This required setting is the name of the post type you're creating. Make sure to enter a name that won't conflict with another post type. (The names of custom post types can't be repeated.) The name has be fewer than 20 characters long.

- **Label.** The label of your custom post type is what that post type's section will be called in the navigation bar. (Much like the post types of posts and pages, your custom posts will be displayed in the navigation bar.)

- **Singular Label.** Most post types should be plural because they're collections of similar items. Chances are that you'll have more than one post of a given post type, but if you have only one post of that type, WordPress needs to know what label to display for it.

- **Description.** In this text box, enter a brief description of the custom post type.

You're going to create a custom post type of book, so fill out the form as shown in **Figure 9.3**. If you change your mind later, you can click the Reset link at the top of the form to clear any values you've entered.

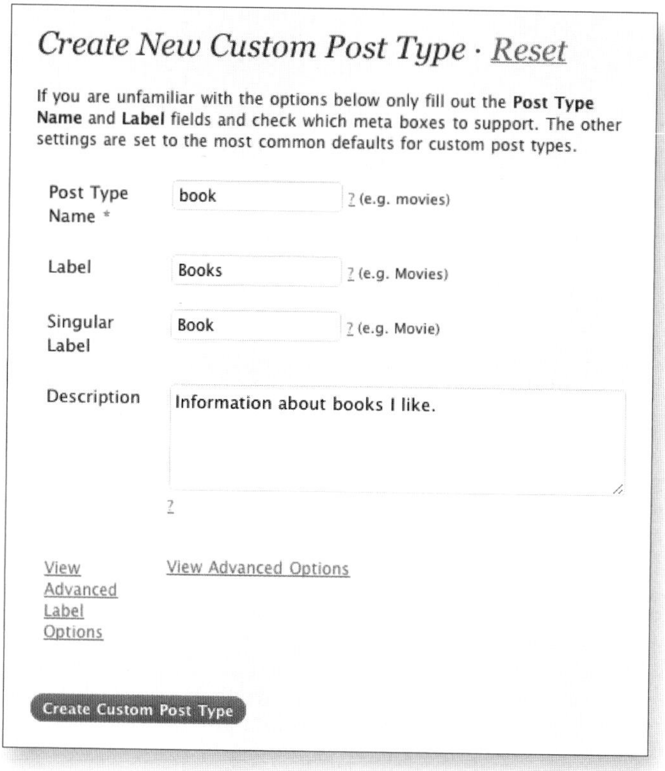

Create New Custom Post Type · Reset

If you are unfamiliar with the options below only fill out the **Post Type Name** and **Label** fields and check which meta boxes to support. The other settings are set to the most common defaults for custom post types.

Post Type Name *	book	? (e.g. movies)
Label	Books	? (e.g. Movies)
Singular Label	Book	? (e.g. Movie)
Description	Information about books I like.	
	?	
View Advanced Label Options	View Advanced Options	

Create Custom Post Type

Figure 9.3 Creating a custom post type of book.

Clicking the View Advanced Options link displays a few more options that you can specify for your custom post type (**Figure 9.4**).

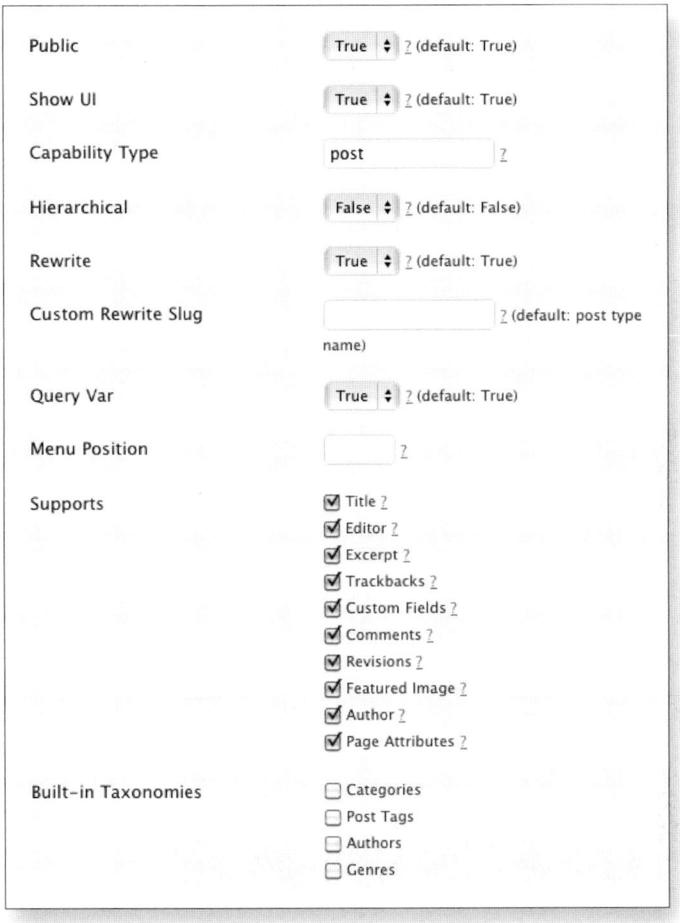

Public	True ⬍ ? (default: True)
Show UI	True ⬍ ? (default: True)
Capability Type	post ?
Hierarchical	False ⬍ ? (default: False)
Rewrite	True ⬍ ? (default: True)
Custom Rewrite Slug	? (default: post type name)
Query Var	True ⬍ ? (default: True)
Menu Position	?
Supports	☑ Title ? ☑ Editor ? ☑ Excerpt ? ☑ Trackbacks ? ☑ Custom Fields ? ☑ Comments ? ☑ Revisions ? ☑ Featured Image ? ☑ Author ? ☑ Page Attributes ?
Built-in Taxonomies	☐ Categories ☐ Post Tags ☐ Authors ☐ Genres

Figure 9.4 The advanced options give you much more control of your new custom post type.

You should keep most of the default settings, but the following two options will help you further customize your post type:

- **Menu Position.** This option determines where in the navigation bar your custom post type module appears. If you want it to appear at the top of the navigation bar, enter 1 in the text box. If you don't enter anything, your new custom post type will be listed at the bottom of the second navigation bar (the one that lists posts, pages, and the like).

- **Supports.** This option is where you get the most bang for your buck in customizing your custom post type. Each of the items listed in the Supports section also appears in the New Post and New Page screens (as well as in their respective edit screens). If the box next to an item is checked, that item will appear in the edit and new screens of your custom post type. The book type doesn't need to list an excerpt, trackbacks, custom fields, comments, revisions, or page attributes, so clear those check boxes (refer to Figure 9.4).

When you're happy with your settings, click the Create Custom Post Type button. The plug-in creates your custom post type while you wait. (Don't worry; the wait isn't long at all.)

When you refresh your browser, you should see a new entry in the navigation bar: Books (**Figure 9.5**). The Books link takes you to a screen listing all the book posts you have on your blog (at the moment, none, because you just created the post type), and the Add Book link takes you to the Add New Book screen.

Figure 9.5 Your new custom post type (book) appears in the navigation bar like a native feature of WordPress.

Now click the Add Book link to check out the Add New Book screen (**Figure 9.6**). This screen is a simplified version of the standard Add New Post screen, showing the items that you chose in the advanced options section of the Add New screen (refer to Figure 9.4).

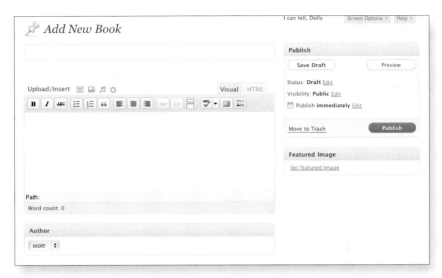

Figure 9.6 The Add New Book screen.

Just fill in the information as you normally would and click Publish to create your first post of your custom post type.

Understanding post-type permalinks

After you add a new post that has a custom post type, it doesn't appear in your blog's index. The default WordPress theme (like most all other themes) displays only posts with the post type of post. To have other post types appear in the index, you have to edit your theme, as I explain in Chapter 13.

The post you created does exist, however, and you can get to it even if it isn't displayed on your main page. In the example in this chapter, you created a post with a custom type of book for the very book you're reading. (Freaky, huh?) If you go into your custom post type's edit screen (by clicking your custom post type in the navigation bar), you'll see a button called View *x*, where *x* is whatever you've named your post type. For this example, the button is called View Book (**Figure 9.7**).

Figure 9.7 The View Book button takes you to your custom post.

Click that button to view your post, and make note of the URL, which will look like this:

http://*yourwordpressURL.com/yourCustomPostTypeName/Title_of_Post*

For the book post-type example, the URL of the post for this book would be

http://www.ipadbungalow.com/book/building-a-wordpress-blog-people-want-to-read/

As you can see, your custom post type's name is important because it becomes part of the permalink for each post with that post type. Keep this in mind when you're creating post types.

Creating a custom taxonomy for a post type

You have a custom post type of book, and now you want to be able to associate those posts with their authors and genre. This is a job for custom taxonomies.

In the Custom Post Type UI plug-in, click the Add New link in the navigation bar. When the Add New screen opens, you see the Create Custom Taxonomy section on the right side of the screen (refer to Figure 9.2).

For this example, fill out the form as follows:

- **Taxonomy Name.** Enter **book_authors** in this text box. You may wonder why I'm not having you call the taxonomy *authors*. I was tempted to, but because WordPress itself tracks authors, I thought it best to prefix the taxonomy name with the post type it will be describing—generally a good practice to avert any naming conflicts within WordPress.

- **Label.** The label is what will be displayed in the post, so entering **Authors** is fine here.

- **Singular Label.** For the single label, as you might expect, just enter **Author**.

- **Attach to Post Type.** The final section, which is required, tells WordPress which post type should have this custom taxonomy available to it. You can choose more than one post type to make sure of your custom taxonomies, and you can even apply them to the stock post and page post types. In this case, select the Books check box to apply the taxonomy to the book post type—the type I just created.

Figure 9.8 shows what your settings should look like at this point.

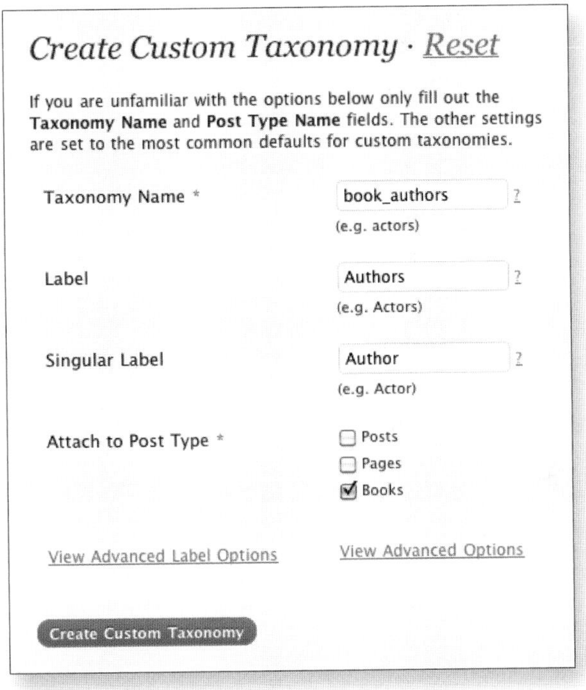

Figure 9.8 Creating a custom taxonomy with the Custom Post Type UI plug-in.

When all the options are set, click the Create Custom Taxonomy button.

In addition to creating the Authors custom taxonomy, you just created a Genres taxonomy. The Books module in the navigation bar now lists both Authors and Genres links (**Figure 9.9** on the next page). Clicking the link for your custom taxonomy (in this case, either Authors or Genres) takes you to the management screen for that taxonomy, which behaves just like the category-management screen that I cover in Chapter 6.

Figure 9.9 The custom taxonomies Authors and Genres are now listed in the Books module.

Click Add Book (or whatever your custom post type is) to see the other way you can add entries to your custom taxonomies. Two new modules appear for the book custom post type: Authors and Genres (**Figure 9.10**). Add entries to the custom taxonomies associated with your custom post types the way you'd add tags to a post: Enter as many terms as you like in the appropriate field (Authors or Genres, in this case), separating terms with commas, and then click Add to add the new entries to the custom taxonomy.

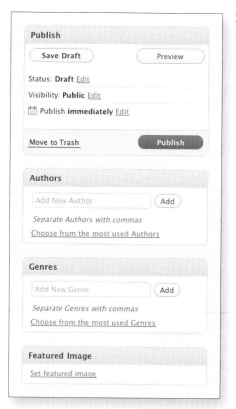

Figure 9.10 Custom taxonomy fields appear in the new/edit screen of the post type they're associated with.

When you view the post, your custom taxonomy entries don't show up. This is another template issue, and I show you how to correct it in Chapter 13.

Some Uses for Custom Post Types and Taxonomies

By now, I hope your mind is buzzing with potential ways to leverage both of these features in your blog. If not, here are a couple of simple ways to use custom post types and taxonomies:

- **Rudimentary store displays.** Create a custom post type for each type of item (pants, shirts, what have you), and use custom taxonomies to list the sizes, prices, and colors available.

- **Photos.** If you're a photographer, you may want to post pictures and not deal with any of the other standard post types. Just create a custom post type of picture, and use a custom taxonomy to track exposure and other camera settings.

- **Events.** If you hold classes or other events, you can create a custom post type of event to display them in your blog's sidebar. The custom taxonomies could include the dates and locations of the events.

10

Handling Links

Posts and pages are like fraternal twins. They have many similar traits, but they aren't exact copies. Links are the red-headed stepchildren of the WordPress family. (No offense intended to you actual red-headed stepchildren out there; I'm sure you're fantastic people.) Links bear very little relation to pages and posts. Sure, the interface for managing them is pretty much the same, but links serve a very different purpose from either posts or pages.

In this chapter, I define what links are, show you how to add them to your blog, and go over how to manage your collection of links. I also cover link categories and give you a few ideas on how to use links on your blog.

What the Heck Are Links?

Way back in the early days of blogging (way, way back in the ancient times of 1999), the blogosphere was a small place. A few bloggers linked to one another, and everyone liked this arrangement. Then the introduction of easily installable blogging solutions (like WordPress) opened blogging to a whole new set of people. These people were reading more and more blogs, and they wanted a way to share all the cool blogs they were tracking with their audiences. The blogroll was born, and the Internet has never been the same.

At its core, a *blogroll* is a list of links, usually displayed in a *sidebar* (a column of a blog that doesn't contain the blog's main content, usually located on the right side of the page). Fancier blogrolls incorporate pictures and perhaps a link to the blog's feed.

Maintaining blogrolls by hand was laborious, so WordPress added links to the mix. That's why when you check out the prepopulated links in the Links module in the left navigation bar of the Dashboard, you find all of them in one category: Blogroll.

Although the links feature of WordPress was designed to display your blogroll, you don't have to limit yourself to that function. You can also use links to organize and display any sort of link list. Have a bunch of favorite Web comics that you like? Create a Web Comics link category, with a link to each comic. Want to use links for a blogroll but organize the blogroll by type? Because WordPress doesn't apply the subcategory concept to links, create a category for each type and then assign blogs to the right categories (**Figure 10.1**).

Figure 10.1 Two groups of links in two different categories.

Typically, links are grouped by category when they're displayed on a blog page. You can add as many categories as you want to organize your links (such as Awesome Web Sites in Figure 10.1), but you can't delete the Blogroll category.

tip If you don't want to use the Blogroll category, you can rename it or take all the links out of it. See "Editing and deleting links" later in this chapter for more information.

Configuring Links

Now that you know what links are and why they're an option in WordPress, I'll talk about how to add, edit, and delete them. Much like posts and pages, links are best when they're kept fresh with a little tending and pruning.

Adding links

To add links, click the Links module in the left navigation bar; then click Add New to open the Add New Link screen (**Figure 10.2**).

Figure 10.2 Enter links in this screen.

The first group of settings is pretty basic. Enter the following information about your link:

- **Name.** Enter the text of your link in the Name text box. Normal linking-text best practices apply: Make the text descriptive so that people can get an idea of what the link is without having to click it.

- **Web Address.** In this text box, type the URL of the site you want to link to.

 note   The Web Address entry must include http:// or https://.

- **Description.** In your travels on the Web, you've hovered over a link or two; we all have. Sometimes, some text pops up under your hovering mouse pointer, giving you a little more information about the link. What you enter in the Description text box (an optional setting) is what users see when they hover over the link.

- **Categories**. A link can have as many, or as few, categories as you want to give it. To add a category, click the Add New Category link.

 note   Link categories and post categories are two separate entities, and never the twain shall meet. They're managed and added separately.

The second group of settings in the Add New Link screen—Target and Link Relationship (**Figure 10.3**)—is slightly more advanced.

Both of these settings are optional, but you should know what they do:

- **Target.** Select a Target radio button to control how the linked URL opens. _blank opens a new browser window when the link is clicked, _top opens the linked URL in the full browser window (this behavior is obvious only when you're using frames; the link opens in a window of its own), and _none opens the linked URL in the current window (or *frameset*).

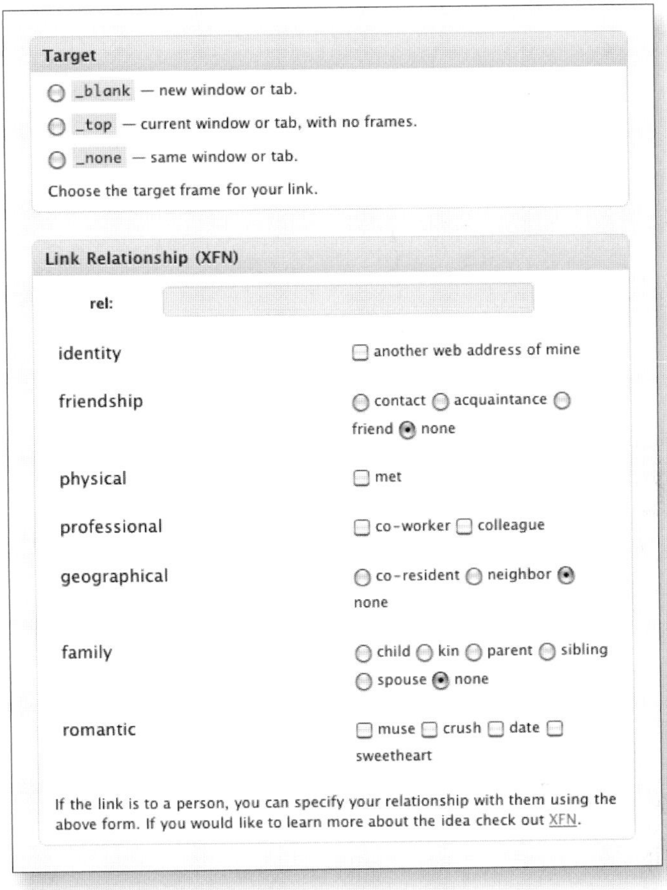

Figure 10.3 Target and Link Relationship are optional settings for your link.

- **Link Relationship (XFN).** I touch on XFN (XHTML Friends Network) in Chapter 6, but the interface for links is much more useful than the interface for posts.

  The table displays the various relationships that XFN can represent. All the options with radio buttons can have only one value, whereas the options with check boxes allow you to select as many values as you like. If I were linking to my own blog, for example, I'd select Another Web Address of Mine in the Identity row and leave it at that. If I were linking to my significant other's blog, however, I'd select Friend in the Friendship row, Met in the Physical row, Co-Resident in the Geographical row, and Sweetheart in the Romantic row (isn't that just too sweet?).

Working with advanced settings

The Advanced settings in the Add New Link screen (**Figure 10.4**) are what
I call super-advanced options. I'll bet that they were reverse-engineered
from alien technology.

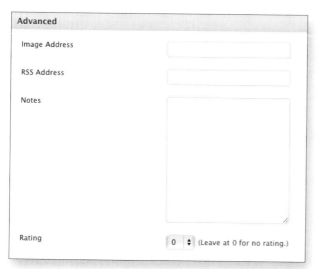

Figure 10.4
The advanced
options are very,
very advanced.

In addition to being super-advanced, these options are very optional. Here's
what you can do with them:

- **Image Address.** Some themes are designed to show an image next to
  the text of the link. (A good image for this purpose is a *favicon*—a little
  icon that people can make for their Web sites; see the following tip.) If
  you want to associate an image with the link, enter the image's URL in
  this text box.

> **tip** Find out more about favicons, and make one for your blog, by
> visiting Steve DeGraeve's Favicon Generator at www.degraeve.
> com/favicon.

- **RSS Address.** In this text box, enter the address of the Web site's syndication feed. If you're linking to another WordPress blog, this URL usually
  is www.*blogname.com*/feed (replacing *blogname.com* with the URL of
  the blog in question, of course).

  For details on RSS, see the nearby sidebar "On Syndication Feeds."

On Syndication Feeds

There are a few competing formats in the blogfeedsphere. The two major flavors are Atom and RSS 2.0. (*RSS* stands for *Really Simple Syndication*.) WordPress supports both formats out of the box, so you don't need to worry about support issues.

When you're browsing other people's blogs, though, you may wonder why they choose to use a particular format over another. The short answer is this: The blogger isn't choosing; the vendor of his blogging tool is. I'd say that 98 percent of the bloggers out there don't care which format their feeds are in as long as newsreaders can consume them.

Because WordPress supports the two major RSS formats, the vast majority of readers will be able to read your blog.

 note Some themes make it easy for your readers to subscribe to the blogs in your blogroll by adding the RSS address to the list (based on the value you enter in the RSS Address text box).

- **Notes.** At first blush, you may think that notes are just like descriptions (which I cover in "Adding links" earlier in this chapter), but they're not. A description is text that pops up when someone hovers a mouse pointer over the link, whereas the text you enter in the Notes box appears on the page below the link (depending on your WordPress theme, that is; see Chapters 12 and 13 for the story on themes).

- **Rating.** You can rate each link from 0 to 10 (0 being no rating and 10 being the highest) by making a choice from the Rating drop-down menu. Most themes don't display rating information, but you can alter a theme to show it (as you can for any of these optional settings), and you can sort links by rating.

Saving your settings

After you've configured all your settings for the link, you need to save those settings. You'll notice a Save module in the top-right corner of the Add New Link screen (refer to Figure 10.2); this module includes a handy-dandy Add

Link button, which you can click to save the link (brilliant!). Right above the Add Link button is a check box titled Keep This Link Private (**Figure 10.5**). If you check that box before you click Add Link, WordPress saves the link but doesn't make it visible on your blog. This feature is useful if you want to use your blog as a repository for links you want to remember but don't necessarily want to share with the public.

Figure 10.5 You can keep a link private, if you want.

Importing Links

If you use a newsreader of any kind, you're familiar with OPML. *OPML* (which stands for *Outline Processor Markup Language*) is an XML format that was originally designed for outlines; newsreader vendors have adopted it as a way to get a list of links exported from an application so that your subscription list becomes portable.

It stands to reason that any links you'd want to include in the sidebars of your blog would be in your newsreader, which in turn can export them to an OPML file. WordPress will happily import that OPML file and add those links to your blog. Before you can start using this method to import links, though, you need to have an OPML file on your computer or somewhere on the Internet. You also need to know where that file is so you can supply the location to the Blogroll importer.

To use this feature, first you need to install the Blogroll importer plug-in. Follow these steps:

1. Click Tools in the administrative interface's navigation bar.

2. Click Import.

   You see all the available import plug-ins for WordPress.

3. Click Blogroll.

The Install Importer screen opens (**Figure 10.6**).

Figure 10.6 The Install Importer screen.

4. Click the Install Now button.

5. When the plug-in is installed, click the Activate Plugin & Run Importer link (**Figure 10.7**).

Figure 10.7 The Blogroll importer screen.

The Import Your Blogroll from Another System screen opens (**Figure 10.8** on the next page). Now you're ready to import some links.

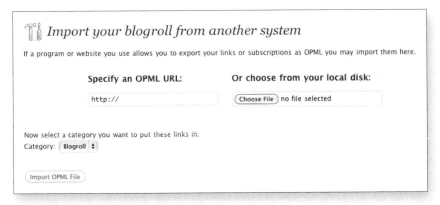

Figure 10.8 Import some links through this screen.

 note   **You need an OPML file to import from.**

6. Type the URL of the OPML file in the Specify an OPML URL text box, or click the Choose File button to find and select an OPML file that you've saved on your computer.

7. From the Category drop-down menu, choose the link category that you want the imported links to go into.

 tip   **Personally, I put all these links in the Blogroll category.**

8. Click the Import OPML File button.

   WordPress imports all your links. When it's done, it displays the link names and indicates whether they were inserted (**Figure 10.9**).

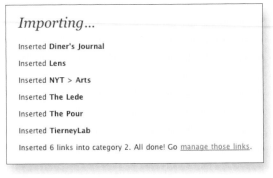

Figure 10.9 Importing is all done!

To manage your newly imported links, click the Manage Those Links link. In the next section, I give you some management tips.

Managing Links

As you might expect, you manage links in the Links screen, which is very similar to the Posts screen. You get to the Links screen by clicking Links in the admin navigation bar.

Viewing all your links

The Links screen displays all the links in your blog in a table (**Figure 10.10**).

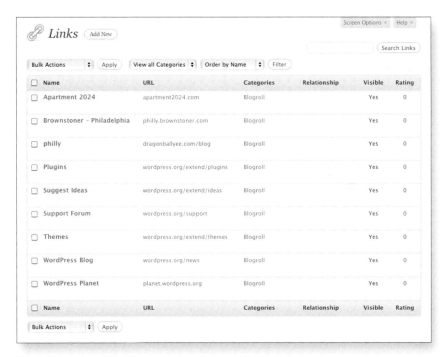

Figure 10.10 Imported links are also displayed in the Links screen.

This table contains the following columns:

- **Name.** Edit a link's information by clicking its name.
- **URL.** This column contains a live link to the site in question.

- **Categories.** This column lists all the categories that a link falls into.

- **Relationship.** The Relationship column contains any XFN data that you entered for this link (refer to "Adding links" earlier in this chapter).

- **Visible.** The setting in this column tells you whether the link is private or public (refer to "Saving your settings" earlier in this chapter).

- **Rating.** The rating you assigned to this link, if any, is displayed here.

Filtering links

As you can in all the other WordPress management screens, you can apply filters in the Links screen to make finding the link you're looking for easier. Just make the appropriate choices from the Category and Order By drop-down menus at the top of the screen.

You can order the results in four ways:

- Order by Link ID
- Order by Name

- Order by Address
- Order by Rating

 note   **Link ID is a unique number that WordPress assigns to each link. This option strikes me as being fairly useless, though.**

After you've picked your filter poison, click the Filter button. Then marvel as WordPress displays only the links that you want to see.

Editing and deleting links

Deleting links is just like deleting posts and pages (processes that I cover in Chapter 7 and Chapter 8, respectively). Click the check box next to the link that you want to delete (or Shift-click to select contiguous links); then choose Delete from the Bulk Actions drop-down menu, and click the Apply button. Those links are gone. You can also delete a link by hovering over it and clicking the Delete link that appears.

Editing links is also quite similar to the posts/pages process. Click the name of the link you want to edit, change the options in the editing screen, and then click the Save button.

Categorizing links

Because posts and pages are very different elements, you'll want to organize your links differently. WordPress makes this process easy by separating post and page categories from link categories.

Viewing link categories

Click Link Categories in the admin navigation bar to open the Link Categories screen (**Figure 10.11**), which has two sections: Add Link Category and a list of your current link categories.

Figure 10.11 Link categories.

note You can't filter these results, so if you have loads of link categories, you may have to do a little bit of scrolling to find the category you're after.

Along with the category name and description, WordPress displays the number of links in each category. Clicking the number in the Links column takes you to the Links screen (refer to Figure 10.10), which applies a filter to show only the links in that category.

Deleting a link category

Deleting a link category is straightforward. Just hover your mouse over the name of the category you want gone, and click the Delete link. (You also see a Quick Edit option in the list of links that appears when you hover.) You can't delete the Blogroll category, but you can change its name if you'd rather use that category for a different set of links.

Adding a link category

You can add as many link categories as you like. Just fill in the following options in the Link Categories screen:

- **Link Category Name.** What you enter in this text box is what WordPress displays as the category name in your links sidebar (depending on your blog's theme).

- **Link Category Slug.** This entry is the URL-friendly version of the category name. Permalinks (see Chapter 5) are based on this slug, so use only lowercase letters, numbers, and hyphens.

- **Description.** Description is the only optional setting. You can enter a description of the link in this text box, but keep it short: Some themes display the description, and overly long descriptions could unbalance the aesthetics of your theme.

When you're done, click the Add Category button (or the Edit Category button, if you're working with an existing link) to save your work and create or edit the link information.

11

Coping with Comments

I've covered a few ways for you to create content for your blog: posts, pages, and links. The final piece of the content puzzle is comments.

Comments are a little unusual. You can leave comments on your blog, and so can other people (assuming that you allow comments at all), which means that you have no idea what content other people will create in your blog. Before you freak out, worry not—WordPress offers robust comment management tools that help you separate the wheat from the chaff.

Comments: Bad or Good?

The first decision to make about comments is whether you even want to allow them in your blog. By default, WordPress enables comments globally, but this setting is simple enough to change. Choose Settings > Discussion to open the Discussion Settings screen, and take a look at the first four sections: Default Article Settings, Other Comment Settings, E-Mail Me Whenever, and Before a Comment Appears (**Figure 11.1**). In the Default Article Settings section, clear the Allow People to Post Comments on New Articles check box.

Default article settings	☑ Attempt to notify any blogs linked to from the article.
	☑ Allow link notifications from other blogs (pingbacks and trackbacks.)
	☑ Allow people to post comments on new articles
	(These settings may be overridden for individual articles.)
Other comment settings	☑ Comment author must fill out name and e-mail
	☐ Users must be registered and logged in to comment
	☐ Automatically close comments on articles older than 14 days
	☑ Enable threaded (nested) comments 5 levels deep
	☐ Break comments into pages with 50 top level comments per page and the last page displayed by default
	Comments should be displayed with the older comments at the top of each page
E-mail me whenever	☑ Anyone posts a comment
	☑ A comment is held for moderation
Before a comment appears	☑ An administrator must always approve the comment
	☑ Comment author must have a previously approved comment

Figure 11.1 The Default Article Settings and Other Comment Settings sections of the Discussion Settings screen give you total control of who can comment on your blog.

note If you decide to disable comments globally, you can still enable comments on a post-by-post basis, as I explain in more detail in Chapter 6.

The downside of comments

Why disable comments? Comment spam is the biggest reason. Comment spam, much like normal email spam, attempts to use your blog to advertise a variety of things and to provide links to sites that you probably don't want to be associated with. You can combat this scourge in ways that don't take all the fun of commenting away, however; I talk about those techniques in "Dealing with Comment Spam" later in this chapter.

The other main reason for disabling comments is simple: You aren't interested in what your readers have to say. Some people view a blog as a bully pulpit; their blogs exist only to distribute their messages and don't need to be mucked up with random comments from every Tom, Dick, or Harry.

The upside of comments

The arguments against comments have their place, but I suggest that you think long and hard about the kind of place you want your blog to be. I find that the blogs I enjoy visiting most have a conversational tone, which is enhanced by the opportunity to leave comments and to interact with the poster and fellow readers alike.

Also, blogging is far more interesting when other people comment on your work, because commenting on your own posts is akin to having a discussion with yourself while looking into a mirror. Sure, it's fun for a few minutes, but after a while, you get to thinking that there's more to life than your deep, deep blue eyes.

Deciding Who Can Comment

Assuming that I've persuaded you to let people comment on your blog, you have a second decision to make: Which members of the unwashed masses should be able to post a comment on your blog?

Out of the box, WordPress lets anyone comment on your blog, but if that setting is just a little too wide open for your comfort, you can restrict commenting access to those folks who have user accounts on your blog. To restrict comments to users, choose Settings > Discussion to open the Discussion Settings screen (refer to Figure 11.1). In the Other Comment Settings section, check the box titled Users Must Be Registered and Logged in to Comment; then click the Save Changes button at the very bottom of the screen. This method is an effective means of combating comment spam, and it lowers the risk that people will leave nasty comments on your posts.

This approach has one obvious downside, however: With everyone already having so many accounts and passwords to remember, do you really want to add that extra layer to enable commenting on your blog? You're sure to lose some commenters who aren't interested in signing up for an account just to leave a comment (though the counterargument also stands: If that person's comment isn't worth the effort of creating an account for, it probably isn't worth having).

I'm a proponent of having a devil-may-care attitude toward comments. Let everyone comment; then install a plug-in or two that makes comment spam much more manageable (as I discuss at the end of this chapter). But it's your blog, of course, so it's your choice.

Understanding How Users Comment

Before I delve into how you edit, delete, and generally manage comments in the back end of your blog, I'll explain how people leave comments in the first place.

How unregistered users comment

Figure 11.2 shows a typical comment form for unregistered users of your blog.

Leave a Reply

Your email address will not be published. Required fields are marked *

Name *

Email *

Website

Comment

You may use these HTML tags and attributes: `<a href="" title=""> <abbr title=""> <acronym title=""> <b> <blockquote cite=""> <cite> <code> <del datetime=""> <em> <i> <q cite=""> <strike> <strong>`

Post Comment

Figure 11.2 The Leave a Reply form for unregistered users in the default WordPress theme.

Each comment form has four elements:

- Commenter's name

- Commenter's email address

- URL of commenter's Web site (if any)

- Comment text

The Name and Email settings are required (though by default, WordPress doesn't display commenters' email addresses). This identification require-ment is yet another arrow in your quiver for use against nasty comments; when people have to include their names with their comments, they may be more polite. To change this requirement, choose Settings > Discussion to open the Discussion Settings screen; in the Other Comment Settings section, clear the check box titled Comment Author Must Fill out Name and E-Mail; then click the Save Changes button. When this box is checked, a commenter must enter both her name and email address; when it's cleared, the commenter doesn't have to enter either piece of information.

note If you check the check box titled Comment Author Must Have a Previously Approved Comment in the Before a Comment Appears section (refer to Figure 11.1), anyone who's had a comment approved in the past gets a free pass whether or not he's a registered user; his comment skips moderation.

To submit the completed form, the user simply clicks the Post Comment button in the Leave a Reply screen.

When users are required to provide both their names and email addresses, and someone tries to enter a comment without providing that information, WordPress displays an error message. WordPress also displays error messages when a user tries to submit a blank comment or submits several comments in rapid succession—behaviors that are typical of programs that leave comment spam. That user is blocked for a few minutes; when that period is up, the user can comment again.

How registered users comment

If a logged-in registered user wants to comment, he sees a slightly different comment form (**Figure 11.3**). All he has to do is enter his comment in the text box and click the Post Comment button. Because the user is already logged in, WordPress already knows who he is, so it doesn't need to ask for identity information again.

Leave a Reply

Logged in as <u>scott</u>. <u>Log out?</u>

Comment

You may use these <u>HTML</u> tags and attributes: `<a href="" title=""> <abbr title=""> <acronym title=""> <b> <blockquote cite=""> <cite> <code> <del datetime=""> <em> <i> <q cite=""> <strike> <strong>`

(Post Comment)

Figure 11.3 The Leave a Reply form for logged-in users.

tip   A logged-in user can click his name in the comment form to edit his profile information (see Chapter 3).

Moderating Comments

After a user submits a comment, depending on the blog's settings, either she sees her comment on the post along with the message *Your comment is awaiting moderation* (**Figure 11.4**), or the comment is published immediately.

You may wonder how WordPress can display a comment that is awaiting moderation to the person who left it while hiding it from everyone else. The answer is quite simple: magic. OK, not really, but it seems like magic, doesn't it? WordPress uses browser cookies to keep track of who is looking at the blog. Thanks to the cookies, WordPress can display certain content, such as comments, to certain people.

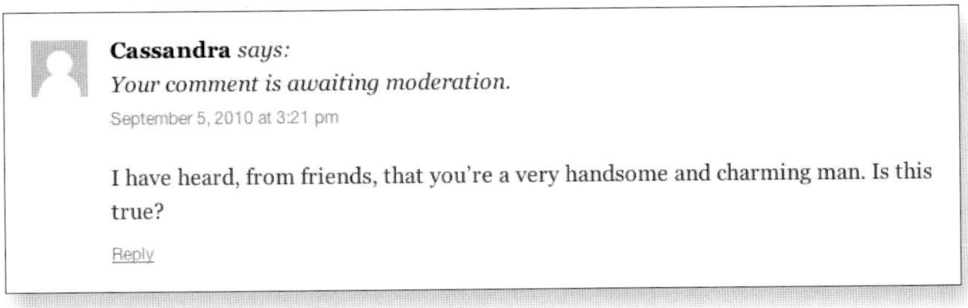

Cassandra *says:*

Your comment is awaiting moderation.

September 5, 2010 at 3:21 pm

I have heard, from friends, that you're a very handsome and charming man. Is this true?

Reply

Figure 11.4 A posted comment awaiting moderation. And yes, Cassandra, that is true.

Moderation is your job as an administrator, as I discuss in the following sections.

Comment tests

Before you see any comments, WordPress tests all comments that people submit to your blog based on the following information:

- **Identity requirements.** I discuss these settings in "How unregistered users comment" earlier in this chapter.

- **Comment contents.** WordPress also considers the comment moderation settings in the Discussion Settings screen. (For a full discussion, see "Comment moderation" in Chapter 5.)

- **Blacklist.** WordPress checks to see whether the comment is spam based on the blacklist settings in the Discussion Settings screen. (The "Comment blacklist" section in Chapter 5 has the full story on these settings.)

note Depending on what plug-ins you have installed, those plug-ins may also scan comments before they are cleared or marked as spam. (See Chapter 14 for more information about plug-ins.)

If a comment passes all these tests, WordPress sends it to the moderation queue and alerts you (as the administrator) that the comment is waiting for moderation.

Comment alerts

When WordPress sends a comment to moderation, it's asking a human (that is, an Administrator user of the blog) to look at the comment and give it thumbs-up or thumbs-down. By default, WordPress sends you, via email, the text of each comment that ends up in the moderation queue.

The email that you receive is pretty darned concise and useful. The post title is in the Subject line of the email, along with the phrase *Please moderate* (which allows you to create some mail rules to organize your email, if that's your bag).

The body of the message includes a link to the blog post that received the comment, as well as some information about the comment (**Figure 11.5**):

Figure 11.5 A typical comment-notification email, viewed in Gmail.

- **Author.** This line lists the comment's author, the IP address of the computer he sent the comment from, and a reverse lookup on that address.

- **E-Mail.** This line provides the commenter's email address, if you require it (refer to "How unregistered users comment" earlier in this chapter).

- **URL.** If the commenter provided a URL, it appears in this line.

- **Whois.** This line is link to a Whois lookup on the commenter's IP address, which returns some information about the commenter's location.

- **Comment.** This line contains the comment text.

You can disable, or enable, these notifications by choosing Settings > Discussion to open the Discussion Settings screen (refer to Figure 11.1). In the E-Mail Me Whenever section, you'll see two options: Anyone Posts a Comment and A Comment Is Held for Moderation. By default, both boxes are checked, which means that an email will be sent in both cases. Clear both boxes if you don't want to receive these emails.

Below all that information are four links that let you act on the comment. I discuss these actions in the following sections.

Comment actions

The bottom of a comment-notification email from WordPress provides links to four separate actions you can take on the pending comment, as I discuss in the following sections.

Approve the comment

To approve the comment, click the Approve It link. That link takes you to the Moderate Comment screen (**Figure 11.6**), which asks whether you're sure you want to approve the comment. Click No or Approve Comment. If you click No, the comment remains in the moderation queue.

Figure 11.6 Confirm comment approval in this screen.

Trash the comment

If the comment is obviously spam or is otherwise objectionable, you can move the comment to the trash (effectively deleting it) by clicking the Trash It link at the bottom of the notification email. The Moderate Comment screen asks whether you're sure you want to trash the comment (**Figure 11.7**). Click No to cancel or Trash Comment to proceed.

Figure 11.7 Confirm comment deletion in this screen.

Mark the comment as spam

Instead of deleting a comment outright, you can mark it as spam by clicking the Spam It link in the notification email. Again, the Moderate Comment screen asks you to confirm your choice (**Figure 11.8**); click No or Spam Comment.

Moderate Comment

Caution: You are about to mark the following comment as spam:

Author	Cassandra
E-mail	cassie@test.com
Comment	I have heard, from friends, that you're a very handsome and charming man. Is this true?

Are you sure you want to do this?

No   Spam Comment

Figure 11.8 Confirming that you want to mark a comment as spam.

Unlike deleting a comment, marking a comment as spam doesn't delete it from the WordPress database. Instead, WordPress holds on to the comment in the hope that you'll activate a comment-spam plug-in, so that it can add the comment to a central spam-comment database (see "Dealing with Comment Spam" later in this chapter).

Manage comments

The final link in the email takes to you to the Comments screen, which applies a filter to display only moderated comments. That screen is the topic of the following section.

Managing Comments

All roads lead to comment management, it seems. You can get to the Comments screen in several ways:

- **Right Now module.** When you log in to the Dashboard, by default, you're greeted by the Right Now module, which has a column called Discussion (**Figure 11.9**). Here, you can see how many total comments your blog has (the topmost item in the column), followed by a breakdown of how many of those comments are approved, spam, or waiting for moderation. The number next to each category is the number of comments in that category. Each category is actually a link that, when clicked, opens the Comments screen, filtered to show only the comments in the category you clicked.

Figure 11.9 The Right Now module gives you instant access to comment statistics.

- **Email link.** You can click the moderation-screen link in the comment-notification email (refer to "Comment alerts" earlier in this chapter) to get to the Comments screen.

- **Comments link.** The navigation bar in the administrator interface contains a Comments link that takes you to the Comments screen. When comments are waiting for moderation, a little speech bubble containing the number of waiting comments appears to the right of the Comments link (**Figure 11.10**).

Figure 11.10 A speech bubble alerts to you to new comments.

Viewing comments

Comment management is just like link, post, and page management, in that you do everything through a management screen—in this case, Comments (**Figure 11.11**).

Figure 11.11 The Comments screen looks very much like the Pages and Posts screens.

This screen lists all the comments on your blog in a nice table that contains the following columns by default:

- **Author.** This column lists the name that the commenter entered, as well as her avatar (where appropriate), URL (if entered), email address, and IP address. If you click the URL, it takes you to that commenter's Web site. If you click the email address, a new email window opens. Finally, clicking the IP address shows you all comments on your blog that originated from that address.

- **Comment.** This wide column displays the comment itself and the date when the comment was left. It's also the home of the action links that appear when you hover over a comment.

tip The Comments screen displays 20 comments at a time, but you can customize this number by choosing a different one from the Screen Options drop-down menu in the top-right corner of the screen (not visible in Figure 11.11).

- **In Response To.** In this column, you see the post on which this comment was left, as well as the number of other comments on said post. Clicking the number will display only the comments on that post.

Deciphering the Comments Screen

Astute readers may have noticed that the background of the Comments screen is two different colors in Figure 11.11. The top comment is awaiting moderation, so it has a light yellow background. The alternating yellow and white backgrounds (white for approved comments) help you see easily how many posts you need to approve.

The number of comments awaiting moderation is also displayed at the top of the Comments screen, next to the Pending link. Click that link, and WordPress filters the screen to show only comments that need to be moderated. You can also show all comments or only pending comments, approved, spam, or trashed comments by clicking the appropriate links.

Managing comments in batches

Approving and rejecting comments individually works well enough when you have one or two comments. But what if you have several hundred comments that need to be approved? Just follow these steps:

1. Click the check boxes of the comments on which you want to execute the bulk action (or Shift-click to select contiguous comments).

2. From the Bulk Actions drop-down menu in the top-left corner of the screen, choose the action you want to take on the selected comments: Unapprove, Approve, Mark As Spam, or Move to Trash.

3. Click the Apply button next to the menu.

   WordPress performs the action instantly. Then you can move on to work on the next batch comments.

Managing individual comments

When you hover your mouse over a comment in the Comments screen, a few links show up in an action menu (**Figure 11.12**).

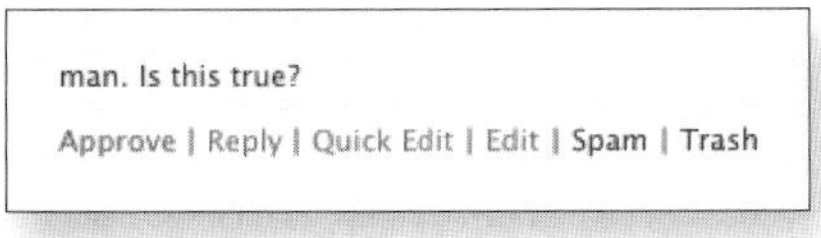

man. Is this true?

Approve | Reply | Quick Edit | Edit | Spam | Trash

Figure 11.12 All the actions you can take on an individual comment.

The available actions are

- **Approve.** If a comment is awaiting moderation, clicking Approve publishes the comment on your blog. (For comments that you've already approved, this link is labeled Unapprove.)

- **Reply.** Blog readers use comments to ask questions of the post's author. As the currently logged-in user, you can reply to any comment by clicking the Reply link. A composition window appears (**Figure 11.13**). Type your comment and click the Submit Reply button, and the comment will be posted.

Figure 11.13 You can reply to comments right from the Comments screen.

- **Quick Edit.** Just like the Quick Edit action-menu link for posts, this link displays a limited editing screen for the selected comment. (See "Editing comments" later in this chapter for the lowdown on the full-featured editor.) Quick Edit allows you to change the name, email address, and URL associated with a comment. You can also change the text of a comment.

- **Edit.** If you need to change the status of a comment, click the Edit link to use the Edit Comment screen.

- **Spam** and **Trash.** I group these two actions together because they both prevent the comment in question from showing up on your blog. Comments should be marked as spam only when they're actually spam comments (see "Dealing with Comment Spam" later in this chapter). Clicking Trash removes the comment from your blog (if it was previously published).

Searching for comments

When you have a large number of comments, searching becomes important. As you can in the management screens for posts, pages, and links, you
can type a search term in the search text box in the top-right corner of the
Comments screen and then click the Search Comments button. WordPress
returns all comments that meet your search criteria (**Figure 11.14**).

Figure 11.14 A search for *test* returns one comment.

Deciphering IP Addresses

You can also click the IP address listed with the comment (see the "Viewing
comments" section earlier in this chapter) to show only comments sent from
the computer with that IP address. This feature is useful when you get
several identical comments from a bunch of seemingly different people.

If you notice a large number of comments coming from the same IP
address but being submitted under different names, one of two things
could be going on:

- Someone is leaving comments under false names.

- Your blog is popular with residents of a single household who use the
  same router to connect to the Internet.

Either way, this is a good trick for figuring out who is leaving comments on
your blog.

Editing comments

Your blog is your kingdom, so you get to make the rules. You decide who can (and can't) comment, post, and otherwise enjoy your blog.

 note Your absolute rule extends to the contents of comments, but a word of warning: With great power comes great responsibility. Why do I mention responsibility? You should think twice before altering words that someone else wrote. Fixing grammatical errors or censoring swear words is one thing, but I, for one, would never want to change the meaning of someone else's comments.

Hover over a comment and click the Edit link in the action menu that appears to get to the Edit Comment screen (**Figure 11.15**), where you can change just about everything related to the comment.

Figure 11.15 Editing a comment. You can change anything you want.

Your options are

- **Name.** You can change the name that the comment was left under by typing a new name in this text box.

- **E-Mail.** You can change the email address associated with a comment as well by typing a new address in this text box. You can also open a new email message in your email client of choice by clicking the Send E-Mail link.

> **note** Most WordPress themes don't display commenters' email addresses in the blog itself so that spambots can't harvest addresses. (For information on themes, see Chapters 12 and 13.)

- **URL.** Type a new address in this text box to change the URL.

- **Comment.** This section is where you enter potentially dangerous territory. You can format the comment by using some familiar HTML tools. (Check out Chapter 6 to find out what these tools do.) You can also change the comment's text, leaving no outward sign that a change has been made.

The Status section has a few more options you can edit for a comment:

- **View Comment.** This button works only for comments that have been approved. Click it to go directly to the comment itself. (Each comment has its own permalink, which is based on the permalink of the post.)

- **Status.** The three options are Approved, Pending, and Spam. To change a comment's status, just select the radio button next to the status you're after.

- **Time.** You can edit the time stamp on the comment by clicking the Edit link next to the time stamp.

- **Move to Trash and Update Comment.** Clicking the Update Comment button saves all your changes; clicking the Move to Trash link moves the comment to the trash. (Trashed comments will not show up on your blog.)

Dealing with Comment Spam

I've mentioned comment spam more than a few times already because it's a big problem. For very little money, people can program small applications called *bots* to search the Internet for blogs and leave comments full of links to various sites of ill repute. Luckily, WordPress now ships with a plug-in that can really help your fight against comment and trackback spam. (For more on trackbacks, check out Chapter 5.)

The Akismet plug-in—made by Automattic, creator of WordPress.com— adds a step to the comment-vetting process. When a comment is submitted to a blog that's running Akismet, the Akismet Web service runs several tests on that comment, comparing it with known spam comments in a large database. These tests run very quickly. Then Akismet marks the comment as spam if it meets the criteria or passes it along to the next step in the comment system. (Depending on how you have your blog set up, that next step usually is the moderation or publishing queue. See Chapter 5 for help on deciding whether to moderate your comments.)

You don't know it yet, but you're going to love this plug-in.

Activating the Akismet plug-in

Activating Akismet is easy. Click Plugins in the WordPress navigation bar and then click the Inactive link at the top of the screen. You'll see two plug-ins listed in the Inactive section of the Plugins screen (**Figure 11.16**). Next to each inactive plug-in, you see three links: Activate, Edit, and Delete. Click Activate in the Akismet row, and the plug-in is activated, but an alert tells you that you must enter your Akismet API key to make it work.

Figure 11.16 Activating Akismet is as simple as clicking the Activate link and providing your API key.

This API (application programming interface) key is a way for the people at Akismet to track the sources of spam comments. Getting a key may seem like an annoyance, but the key is used to log which comments are being reported as spam. This tracking ensures that legitimate comments aren't being identified as spam for nefarious purposes (and vice versa).

 note   **To get an API key, you need to sign up for a profile at WordPress. com. (Don't worry; it's free.) After you get your profile, click Edit Profile, which is listed in the My Account section, which you can access after logging in to WordPress.com with your new profile. This link takes you to your profile on WordPress.com. Your API key (which you shouldn't share with anyone) is listed right below the header Your Profile and Personal Options.**

To enter your API key, just click the new Akismet configuration link that has appeared below the Plugins module in the navigation bar. The Akismet Configuration screen opens (**Figure 11.17**). Then you have one more decision to make: whether you want Akismet to discard spam comments on posts more than a month old. By default, this option is disabled, which means that spam comments on posts older than a month are treated just like any other potential spam comments: marked as spam and held in a queue for 15 days. If you don't mark them as not spam, the comments are deleted after 15 days.

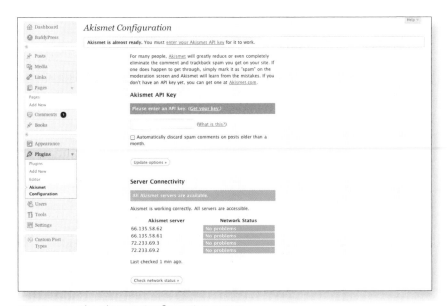

Figure 11.17 The Akismet Configuration screen.

The Cost of Akismet

Akismet is a great plug-in and a bargain at any price, if you ask me. Luckily, Automattic gives Akismet away to the vast majority of users. If you're using Akismet for only one or two blogs, you don't need to pay anything.

A few paid options are available, though, offering the usual benefits:

- Paid accounts have priority over free accounts in the form of getting access to new versions first. Requests for paid accounts are handled by the Web service before free-account requests (though the difference isn't noticeable).

- Traffic is never throttled for paid accounts. The Akismet Web service may check free accounts for spam less frequently, however, if those free accounts generate lots of requests.

- Paid users get notified first when an update is out.

If you make more than $500 a month from your blogs, you may want to opt for a Pro Blogger API key. For $5 a month, you get access to all the benefits I just described, as well as technical support against comment spam.

Enterprise customers (big companies) can sign up for enterprise-level accounts, and discounts are available for not-for-profit organizations.

Check out http://akismet.com/commercial for all the pricing details.

If you change your mind about these settings or want to use your API key for another blog, you can change these settings at any time by choosing Plugins > Akismet Configuration (a command that's available only when the Akismet plug-in is active).

Viewing the spam queue

Click the Spam link at the top of the Comments screen (refer to Figure 11.11) to open the Caught Spam screen, which shows your spam queue. This screen is where you go to see all the spam that has been caught and to make sure that no valid comments have been wrongly accused. The screen shown in **Figure 11.18** on the next page has a bunch of spam comments.

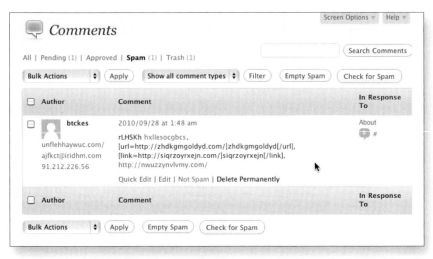

Figure 11.18 The Caught Spam screen.

The handy Empty Spam button deletes every spam comment in the queue, no matter how many there are. WordPress doesn't ask you to confirm each individual deletion, so make sure that you want to delete all the spam comments before you click that button.

You can filter this screen by choosing Show All Comment Types, Comments, or Pings from the Filter drop-down menu and then clicking the Filter button next to it. You can also search your spam queue for any legitimate comments that may have found their way into the wrong virtual neighborhood.

De-spamming messages entails clicking the Not Spam link that appears below each comment or trackback. You can also click Delete Permanently, which does what you think it does.

12

Working with Themes and Widgets

You may have noticed that I've mentioned WordPress themes in the preceding chapters but haven't really explained what they are. Like a clever tech writer, I was saving all that good information for this chapter.

Themes determine the look of your blog and save you the bother of having to deal with most of the code involved—though if you're interested in that sort of thing, WordPress allows you to get your hands into as much code as you like. Most people will be happy keeping the default WordPress theme, which at this writing is known simply as Twenty Ten. (The people behind WordPress have stated a desire to release a new default theme every year, so depending on when you're reading this book, the theme may have changed.)

Viewing the Current Theme

The default download of WordPress includes just one theme: Twenty Ten. To see what themes you have installed, click the Appearance link in the WordPress admin navigation bar. WordPress takes you right to the Manage Themes screen (**Figure 12.1**).

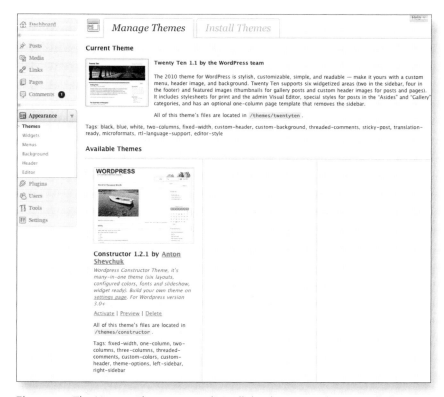

Figure 12.1 The Manage Themes screen lists all the themes you have installed. This example shows a few themes installed in addition to the default theme.

The first thing you see is a thumbnail of the active theme in the Current Theme section (**Figure 12.2**). This theme—the one that's applied to your blog right now—is responsible for the look and feel of your blog. The Current Theme section also displays the theme's name, a link to the author's site, a brief description, and some tags.

Current Theme

Twenty Ten 1.1 by the WordPress team

The 2010 theme for WordPress is stylish, customizable, simple, and readable — make it yours with a custom menu, header image, and background. Twenty Ten supports six widgetized areas (two in the sidebar, four in the footer) and featured images (thumbnails for gallery posts and custom header images for posts and pages). It includes stylesheets for print and the admin Visual Editor, special styles for posts in the "Asides" and "Gallery" categories, and has an optional one-column page template that removes the sidebar.

All of this theme's files are located in `/themes/twentyten`.

Tags: black, blue, white, two-columns, fixed-width, custom-header, custom-background, threaded-comments, sticky-post, translation-ready, microformats, rtl-language-support, editor-style

Figure 12.2 When you're in the Manage Themes screen, finding your current theme is easy.

Viewing the default theme's tags and options

Posts aren't the only things that are tagged in WordPress (see Chapter 6 for more information about tags and posts); themes are also tagged. Unlike a post, though, a theme includes tags to let users know something about the theme without having to apply it.

The default theme, for example, has the following tags: `black`, `blue`, `white`, `two-columns`, `ixed-width`, `custom-header`, `custom-background`, `threaded-comments`, `sticky-post`, `translation-ready`, `microformats`, `rtl-language-support`, and `editor-style`. These tags tell you that that the predominant colors of this theme are black, blue, and white; that you can customize the header and background; that the theme has a fixed width (it doesn't resize with the browser window) and two columns; and that it supports widgets and more.

Some themes have additional options, and WordPress displays links for those options in the Appearance module in the Manage Themes screen's navigation bar (**Figure 12.3**). The default theme, for example, adds options for a custom header and background, which allow you to customize the color of the header graphic and make your blog stand out a little from the crowd.

Figure 12.3 Appearance options in the navigation bar of the Manage Themes screen. Header and Background won't be listed for every theme.

Customizing the default theme's header

The Twenty Ten theme allows you to set a custom header image—
the one that appears at the top of your blog. To customize the header
in the default theme, click the Header link in the Appearance module
(refer to Figure 12.3) to open the Custom Header screen (**Figure 12.4**).

Figure 12.4 The Custom Header screen.

The first section displays a preview of the custom header you're working on. (When you first enter this screen, the currently applied header image is displayed.)

Below the preview section is the Upload Image section, which notes the dimensions of the header image (for the default theme, 940 x 198 pixels). When you upload an image with these dimensions by clicking the Choose File button, selecting an image from your computer, and clicking the Upload button, that image is applied to the header without any changes.

If you upload an image that has dimensions other than 940 x 198, you're taken to the Crop Header Image screen (**Figure 12.5**). Here, you can crop the image to the proper size by moving the dashed-line box to surround the section of the image you want to use. When you're happy with the selection, click the Crop and Publish button, and your new header is live on your blog.

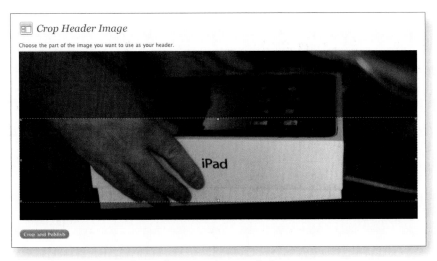

Figure 12.5 Cropping an image has never been easier!

If you aren't interested in uploading a custom image but don't like the default, you can pick another image from the eight images that ship with Twenty Ten. In the Default Images section of the Custom Header screen (refer to Figure 12.4), click the radio button next to the image you'd like to display, and click the Save Changes button at the bottom of the screen. The new header image is set.

Finally, if you change your mind at any time, you can click the Remove Header Image button in the Remove Image section to take the header image off your blog.

note Keep in mind that until you apply a new header image, your blog won't have a header image at all. A safer and more attractive option is to reset the header image to the default by clicking the Restore Original Header Image button in the Reset Image section.

Customizing the default theme's background

The other display option that you can customize is Twenty Ten's background. If you click the Background link in the Appearance module (refer to Figure 12.3), you see the Custom Background screen (**Figure 12.6**).

Figure 12.6 shows the Custom Background screen with a background image already uploaded. To upload a background image, just click the Choose File button in the Upload Image section; browse to the file you want to use; and then click Upload. The image appears in the Preview section at the top of the screen, and some additional display options appear too.

Click the Remove Background Image button to remove the image if you decide that a plain white background is more to your liking (though you can also change the color, as I explain in a moment).

After you've uploaded an image, the Display Options section is where all the action is. This section has four settings:

- **Position.** This setting refers to how the background image is aligned relative to the edge of the browser window. Left, Center, and Right are your three choices. Choose one by clicking the radio button next to it, and notice that the Preview section updates to display the new setting.

- **Repeat.** Do you want your background image to tile over and over again? Maybe you just want to use one row of the image (vertically or horizontally). Or perhaps you've uploaded an image that shouldn't be tiled. The settings in the Repeat section control those functions.

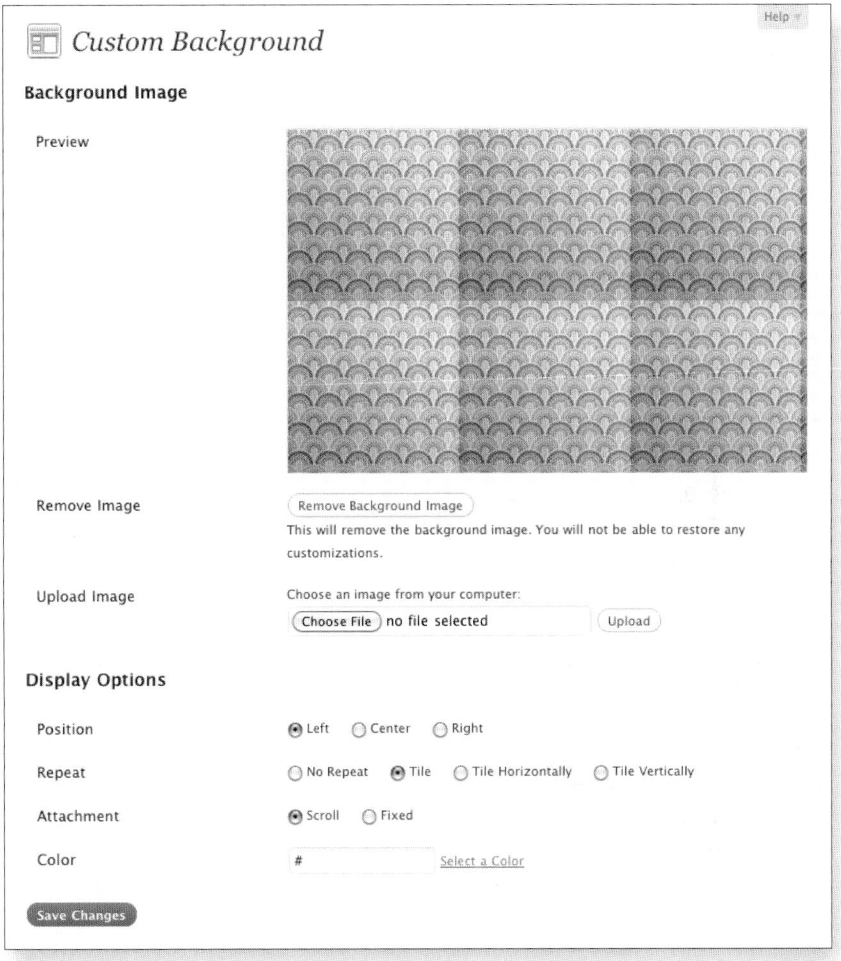

Figure 12.6 The Custom Background screen allows you to apply a custom background to your blog.

- **Attachment.** You have two choices in the Attachment section: Scroll and Fixed. Scroll means that your background will move when a visitor scrolls down on your blog. Fixed means that the image will remain at the top when someone scrolls down (or up!).

- **Color.** You can set the color of your background (by default, it's set to be colorless, which generally translates to white) by clicking the Select a Color link. This link brings up the color selector (**Figure 12.7**), where you can pick a color you like.

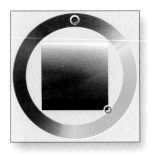

Figure 12.7 Select a color for the background by clicking the middle square and dragging along the circle to find the right hue.

Keep in mind that if you choose to have a background image that repeats and fills the entire background, the color won't be visible. (It'll be under the image.)

Be sure to click Save Changes before you leave the Custom Background screen to apply your changes.

Changing the theme

You don't have to stick with the default WordPress theme, though. You can change your blog's theme in several ways:

- Install and apply a different theme

- Add some widgets (if the theme supports them) to add more content

- Edit the current theme to add or subtract features

In the rest of the chapter, I cover each method in turn. By the end of this chapter, you'll be able to tweak stock themes and make them just what you want.

Installing a New Theme

Every WordPress blog uses the same default theme when it's installed, and this theme is a nice one, but how boring would the blogosphere be if all blogs looked alike? A new theme is like a new coat of paint for your blog, making it stand out from the crowd.

Searching for themes

WordPress has made it easier than ever to find and install themes with a new addition to the Manage Themes screen: the Install Themes tab. When you click it, you're taken to the Install Themes screen (**Figure 12.8**).

Figure 12.8 The Install Themes screen offers you several ways to find a new theme.

This screen offers you a few ways to find a theme you may be interested in:

- **Search.** The Install Themes screen starts you off in the search section. You can search by entering a term like *blue* and clicking the Search button. WordPress will look for the word *blue* in all the relevant data about all the themes in the WordPress Theme Directory, including the theme's name, any tags that may be applied to it (theme builders can tag their themes with descriptive terms), and the author's name.

  You can refine your search by selecting some items in the Feature Filter section. When these filters are applied, the search will return only those themes that include the selected features.

- **Upload.** People make themes available for download across the Web. The Install Themes screen, however, searches only for themes that are listed in the WordPress Theme Directory (http://wordpress.org/extend/themes). What if you want to install a theme that isn't included in that directory? The Upload link allows you to upload theme files to your WordPress installation (as long as all the files are in a .zip archive).

- **Featured, Newest,** and **Recently Updated.** Think of these three options as being "curated" sections—that is, they're selected subsets of the available themes. The Featured section lists themes that were hand-picked by the people who run the WordPress Theme Directory; the Newest and Recently Updated sections showcase the most recently released or updated themes.

Previewing themes

However you search the available themes, the results page that lists all the themes that match your criteria is exactly the same: a grid displaying thumbnails and descriptions of themes (**Figure 12.9**). (If you upload a theme directly, however, you won't see a results page.)

Click either the thumbnail image or the Preview link to preview a theme. This preview, which displays some test content, gives you a good idea of what the theme would look like on your blog (**Figure 12.10**). This feature saves a lot of time when you're trying to decide among several themes. Click the x icon in the top-left corner of the preview window to close it and return to the search-results page.

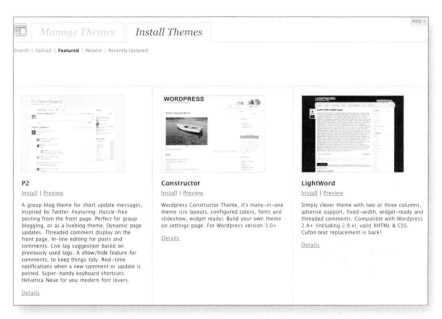

Figure 12.9 Search-results page showing themes that match your search criteria.

Figure 12.10 Clicking a theme's thumbnail or Preview link shows you a preview of that theme.

Installing a theme

When you've found a theme that tickles your fancy, click its Install link. This link (which appears in the search results) opens the theme's Install window (**Figure 12.11**), which tells you a little bit about the theme. To install the theme, click the blue Install Now button.

Figure 12.11 Install the theme by clicking Install Now.

When the theme is installed, you see the installation success screen, as I like to call it (**Figure 12.12**). The Preview link at the bottom of the screen lets you preview the theme again, this time using your blog's content to populate the theme, which gives you a very good idea of how your blog would look with the theme. If you really like the theme, click the Activate link to apply it to your blog, or click the Return to Theme Installer link, which takes you back to the Install Themes screen (refer to Figure 12.9) to search for even more themes.

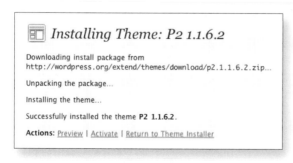

Figure 12.12 When a theme is installed, you can preview or activate it.

Managing Themes

When you have two or more themes installed, you'll probably want to switch among them or perhaps delete themes you no longer want. The Manage Themes screen (refer to Figure 12.1) is where you switch, preview, and delete themes.

Each available theme is presented in the Available Themes section. For each theme, this section provides some information and three options: Activate, Preview, and Delete (**Figure 12.13**). Activate and Preview work just like they do in the installation success screen (refer to Figure 12.12).

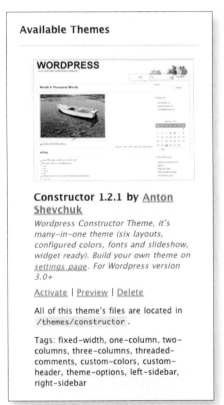

Figure 12.13 A theme's listing in the Manage Themes screen.

The Delete link, as you might guess, allows you to delete the selected theme.

Working with Menus

Every theme includes some built-in menus that are usually generated based on what pages your blog has. (See Chapter 8 for the full story on pages.) The default WordPress theme, Twenty Ten, lists all your pages in its global navigation menu (**Figure 12.14**).

Figure 12.14 The global navigation menu in a blog using the Twenty Ten theme.

Before WordPress 3.0, if you wanted to change that menu or list something other than all your current pages, you had to go mucking around with code. WordPress 3.0, however, introduces the concept of custom menus. In the Appearance module of the admin navigation bar (refer to Figure 12.3), you'll find a link called Menus. Click that link, and you're taken to the Menus screen.

Because this is the first time you're using the Menus screen, it won't list any menus, so you have to make one by using the My Menu module (**Figure 12.15**). Just give your menu a name (like My Menu), and click the Save Menu button.

When you click Save Menu, WordPress does just that, although this new menu has no content and isn't being used on your blog. Also, two new options appear in the My Menu module: Automatically Add New Top-Level Pages and Delete Menu (**Figure 12.16**).

Deleting a menu is straightforward, but what is this top-level-pages business? If you check the box titled Automatically Add New Top-Level Pages, any new page you create that isn't a child page of a top-level page itself will be added to the menu automatically.

After you create your first menu, four other modules appear in the Menus screen. These modules define where the menu appears (Theme Locations) or determine what appears in the menu (Custom Links, Pages, and Categories). I discuss them all in the following sections.

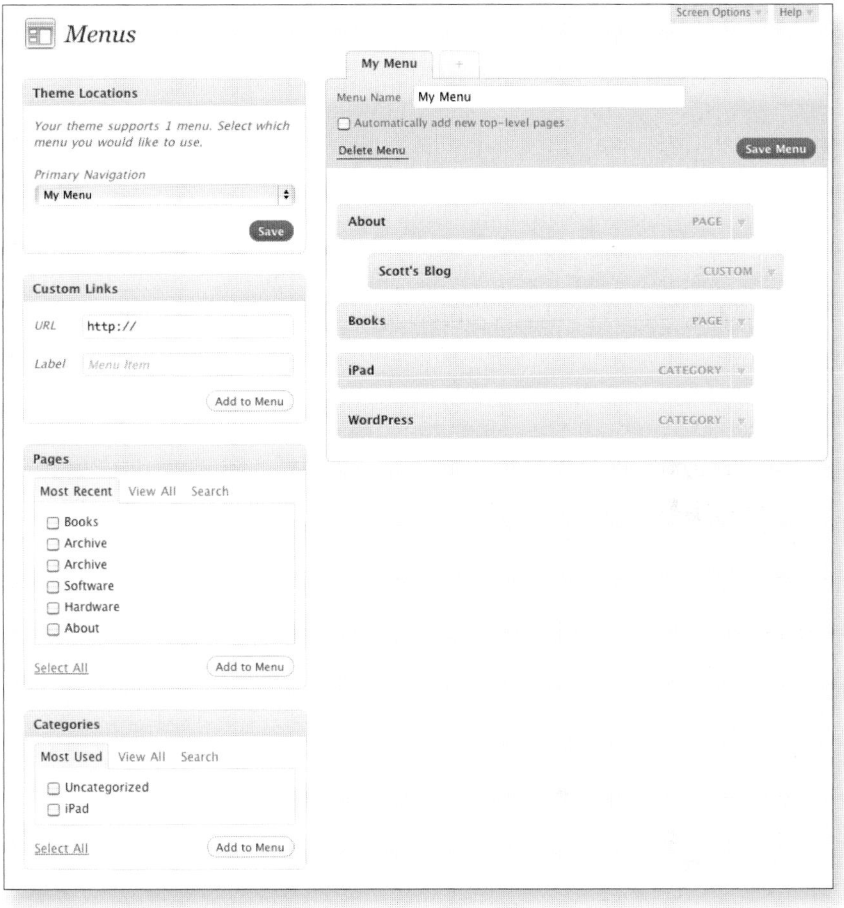

Figure 12.15   The Menus screen, with a custom menu.

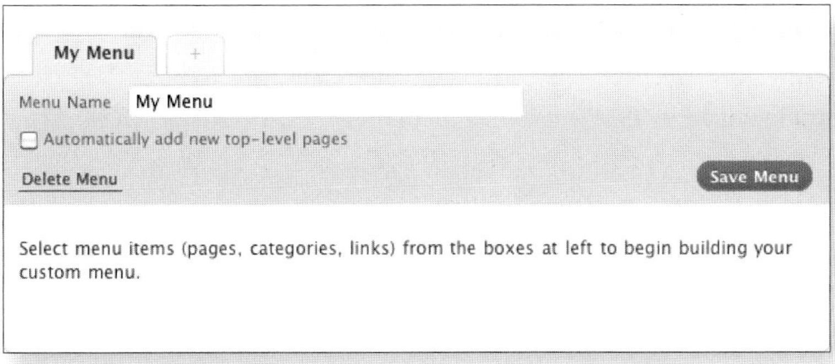

Figure 12.16   A custom menu called My Menu has been created.

Locations, locations, locations

The Theme Locations section of the Menus screen (**Figure 12.17**) gives you some information about your theme and its support for custom menus. In Figure 12.17, you see that Twenty Ten supports only one menu location: the primary navigation menu. Depending on your theme, you may have more options. If you have more than one location, you can create and display more than one custom menu.

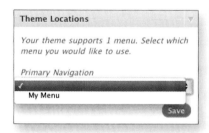

Figure 12.17 The Theme Locations section determines where your menu is displayed.

Setting the menu to display is simple. For each menu location, a drop-down menu lists all the available menus. Choose the menu you want to display in that location, and click Save. Now the menu will appear in that location. You'll probably want to add some content to your menu first, though, as I discuss in the next section.

Content

A menu isn't too exciting until you start adding items to it. You can add three types of things to a custom menu in WordPress, all listed on the left side of the Menus screen (refer to Figure 12.15):

- **Custom Links.** As you might guess, custom links can go anywhere on the Internet. Just enter the URL and the label (which is how the item will appear in the menu), and click Add to Menu (**Figure 12.18**).

Figure 12.18 You can add a link to anywhere to your menu.

- **Pages.** All the pages in your blog are listed in the Pages section (**Figure 12.19**). The Most Recent tab lists pages that were created recently, View All lists all your pages, and Search allows you to search for a particular page. Just check the boxes next to the pages you want to include in your menu and then click Add to Menu.

Figure 12.19 Mix and match your pages here: Display some and don't display others.

- **Categories.** Much as you can with pages, you can display some, all, or none of your categories in your custom menu by making the appropriate selections in the Categories section (**Figure 12.20**) and clicking Add to Menu.

Figure 12.20 Pick the categories you'd like to include in your menu.

When you're added some content, save your menu, and it appears on your blog (**Figure 12.21**).

Figure 12.21 This custom menu is glorious, isn't it?

 tip   **If you have any custom post types or taxonomies (see Chapter 9), they show up as things you can include in a custom menu.**

Menu management

When you have all the content in your menu set, you see something like **Figure 12.22** in the Menus screen. Reordering the content is very easy: Just click and drag the item you want to move to the position you want it to be in.

Figure 12.22 Your menu with all the items in it.

Each item in Figure 12.22 is a menu item, but what if you want to create a submenu? All you have to do is drag and drop the item you want to be a submenu onto the parent menu item. The submenu is indented below its parent menu item.

After you've created a submenu, it appears in your blog in a drop-down menu (**Figure 12.23**). You can even put submenus under submenus below submenus, if you like, to create some rather complicated menus.

About
Books
iPad
WordPress
Scott's Blog

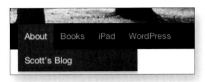

Figure 12.23 A submenu displaying a link to my blog.

Finally, if you decide that you want to change a menu item's label or title attribute (the name of the link that's displayed in the action menu when someone hovers his mouse over that item), just click the title of the item in question to reveal the item's properties (**Figure 12.24**). For pages and categories, you can change the URL, Navigation Label, and Title Attribute settings.

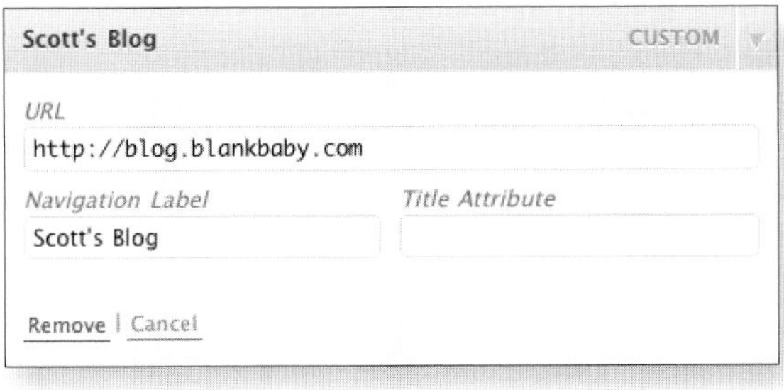
Scott's Blog
CUSTOM
URL
http://blog.blankbaby.com
Navigation Label
Title Attribute
Scott's Blog
Remove | Cancel

Figure 12.24 The properties of a custom link in the Menus screen.

Adding Widgets for Code-Free Customization

If the thought of mucking around with code makes your skin crawl, worry not. Widgets let you customize your WordPress theme without writing a single line of code. Themes that support Widgets have defined areas called *sidebars*. These areas are where you can display widgets on your blog, and those sidebars are displayed in the Widgets screen, which I discuss in the next section.

Viewing widgets

To view your widgets, click the Widgets link in the Appearance module in the navigation bar (refer to Figure 12.3). The Widgets screen opens, listing the widgets that come installed with WordPress (**Figure 12.25**).

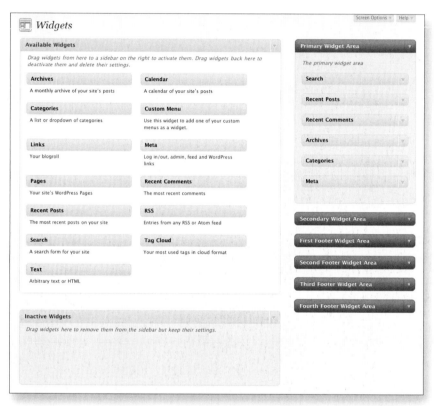

Figure 12.25 The Widgets screen, displaying the default widgets available in a fresh WordPress installation.

As you can see, the Widgets screen lists all the widgets that are installed on your blog. The screen is broken into three sections: Available Widgets, Inactive Widgets, and sidebars. (The sidebars section may vary, depending on the theme you're using.)

Applying widgets

Widgets don't have an installation process of their own, because they're actually specialized plug-ins (or additional parts of traditional plug-ins) that add functions to your sidebar. You install widgets by installing plug-ins that exist solely to add widgets or that have companion widgets in addition to other features. I cover plug-ins in Chapter 14.

To add a widget to the selected sidebar (refer to the preceding section), follow these steps:

1. In the Available Widgets section of the Widgets screen, find the widget you want to use, and drag and drop it onto the sidebar in which you want to display it (**Figure 12.26**).

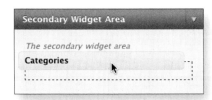

Figure 12.26 Adding the Categories widget to a sidebar.

2. Repeat Step 1 for each widget you want to add.

   You've just added widgets to your blog, and you don't even need to save your changes. The widgets are applied, and saved, as you add them. Not that hard, huh?

Setting widget options

Each widget has some options that change the way it behaves. Changing these options is easy. On the right side of the Widgets screen are the sidebars and all the widgets included in each. You can change the settings only for widgets that are applied to your blog. Click the title bar of the applied widget (it has a little down-pointing arrow on it) that you want to change, and WordPress displays the settings information for that widget. In the following sections, I discuss what each widget does and how you can customize it to suit your needs.

At the very least, you can change the titles of widgets.

Archives

Older entries don't just disappear into the ether; they live on in the archives. The Archives widget (**Figure 12.27**) displays a link to your archives in the sidebar. The archive is shown as a monthly list or as a drop-down menu, and you can display the post count next to the month.

Figure 12.27 The Archives widget.

 tip

If you have a large archive, you may want to check the Display As a Drop Down check box so that the widget takes up less space.

Categories

The Categories widget (**Figure 12.28**) displays all your categories in a list or a drop-down menu. You can also display the number of posts in each category. Finally, if you use parent categories, you can reflect that fact in this widget by enabling the Show Hierarchy option, which indents subcategories below their parent categories.

Figure 12.28 The Categories widget displays categories as links in your sidebar.

Links

The Links widget (**Figure 12.29**) displays a list of your links. You can choose which category of link to show (though you have to show all of them or just one). Click or clear check boxes to show or hide the link's image, name, description, and rating.

Figure 12.29 The Links widget displays all your links and groups them by category.

Pages

If you've created a bunch of pages, the Pages widget (**Figure 12.30**) can display a list of those pages. You can set sorting options and create an *exclusion list* (which allows you to tell the widget which pages you don't want listed). You can also exclude pages based on their IDs; enter those IDs in the Exclude text box, separated by commas.

Figure 12.30 The Pages widget displays your blog's pages based on the criteria you set.

note   To get a page's ID, choose Manage > Pages to open the Pages screen; then click the page's name. At the end of the URL, you see something like post=2. The number is the page's ID number.

Recent Posts

You can showcase as many of your latest posts as you like in your sidebar with the Recent Posts widget (**Figure 12.31**). The widget displays the titles of the posts as links to those posts. You can change the title of this widget.

Figure 12.31 You can set the Recent Posts widget to display up to 15 of your latest posts.

Search

The Search widget (**Figure 12.32**) adds a search control to the sidebar. The only option you can set is the title.

Figure 12.32 The Search widget gives your sidebar a search feature.

Text

The Text widget (**Figure 12.33**) is the most customizable of all. You can enter any text in the body that you want to put in it. You could add a bio of yourself or some code to embed a video, for example. You can also have WordPress add paragraphs to the text automatically, but leave the check box unchecked if you're adding code.

Figure 12.33 The Text widget.

Calendar

Blogs are largely time-based, so it makes sense that you can display a calendar of your posts. The Calendar widget (**Figure 12.34**) allows you to show a month at a time. In the calendar that appears in your blog, each day on which you made a post is a link to that day's posts.

Figure 12.34 The output of the Calendar widget.

Custom Menu

The Custom Menu widget (**Figure 12.35**) lets you display your custom menus in any sidebar. Just select the menu you want to display and click Save, and the menu will be displayed as a set of links, with any hierarchical structure intact.

Figure 12.35 The Custom Menu widget allows you to display any of your custom menus.

Meta

The Meta widget (**Figure 12.36**) displays a collection of links about WordPress itself, including a link to your WordPress login page, a logout link (if you're logged in), and a link to WordPress.org. You can change the display name of this widget, but that's about it.

Meta
- Site Admin
- Log out
- Entries RSS
- Comments RSS
- WordPress.org

Figure 12.36 The Meta widget adds several WordPress-related links.

Recent Comments

As you may have picked up on by this point, I'm a fan of comments. I'm also a fan of the Recent Comments widget, which displays the latest comments that have been left on your blog. **Figure 12.37** shows this widget in action.

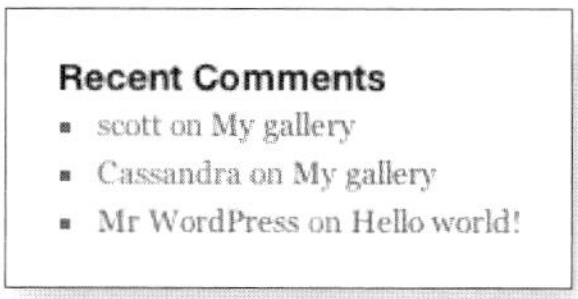

Recent Comments
- scott on My gallery
- Cassandra on My gallery
- Mr WordPress on Hello world!

Figure 12.37 Blogs are conversations, and the Recent Comments widget encourages conversation by highlighting the most recent comments on your blog.

RSS

The RSS widget (**Figure 12.38**) displays the last 1 to 20 posts of a given RSS feed in your sidebar. By default, it shows only headlines that link back to the full post, but you can set it to display item content, item author, and the date of the post.

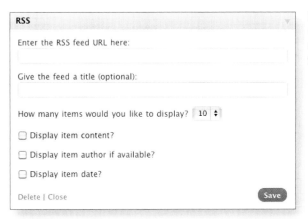

Figure 12.38 The RSS widget displays the contents of any RSS feed that you give it.

Tag Cloud

The Tag Cloud widget is useful only if you tag your posts. (For information on tagging posts, see Chapter 6.) A *tag cloud* is a visual representation of all the tags you use in your blog; the more posts are tagged with a particular word, the larger that word is displayed (**Figure 12.39**). Each tag in the cloud is a link that allows you to search for all posts tagged in that manner. You can change the title of this widget.

Figure 12.39 Tag clouds are all the rage nowadays, and the Tag Cloud widget lets you get in on the fun.

Reordering and removing widgets

Getting rid of a widget that no longer floats your boat is a breeze. Just drag the widget into the Inactive Widgets section of the Widgets screen (refer to Figure 12.25). This action takes the widget off your blog but saves any of the custom settings you applied to it.

You may be happy with the widgets that you have in your sidebar but maybe not with the order in which they appear. To reorder widgets, just drag and drop them into new positions in the Widgets screen's Available Widgets list; then click Save Changes to update your sidebar.

Customizing the Current Theme

Widgets are great ways to make a theme all your own without digging into the actual code of a theme. There are limits to what widgets alone can do, though, and as you become a more advanced WordPress user, you'll run into some of those limits. Luckily, with just a small amount of code editing, you can really change the look and functionality of themes.

Customizing a theme requires you to edit the files that make up the theme itself. You can work with the files in either of two ways:

- Use your favorite text editor to edit the files in the WordPress Theme Directory.

- Use the built-in Theme Editor feature of WordPress to handle the editing duties.

In the following sections, I discuss both methods.

Editing the theme files manually

If you look inside one of your themes' folders, you'll find a variety of files in there. Some, like index.php and page.php, are templates that provide a consistent structure to the content that they display via template tags (which I discuss in Chapter 13). The actual content varies from theme to theme, but most themes have the following basic building blocks:

- **index.php.** This file rules them all. The index file, in Web speak, is the default document. When you visit a Web site (www.wordpressforall.com, for example), what you don't notice is that the Web server is automatically serving up the index.php file. That file contains all the logic needed to present your blog. Without this file, your blog won't work at all. The index.php file contains the logic that controls how your posts are displayed. You can change where the date and author are displayed, tweak the navigation, or have the index display only certain posts by means of a filter.

- **style.css.** You may have .css files in addition to this one, but style.css will definitely be there. CSS (Cascading Style Sheets) uses nifty little text files to specify the physical appearance of your blog. The templates (such as index.php) provide the structure of your blog; CSS provides the paint and wallpaper that make your blog a nice place to hang out.

- **header.php** and **footer.php.** Computers are good at a great many things, chief among them saving us poor saps some time here and there. The pages of your blog have a few common characteristics, including a header graphic, a navigation bar, and a footer with copyright information. The header.php and footer.php files hold header and footer information, respectively. When you need to change either the header or the footer, just edit the appropriate file; WordPress applies the change to your entire blog.

- **page.php** and **single.php.** Both these files are templates for content types. The page.php file is the default page template, and single.php is the template for posts. (Whenever someone visits a post's permalink, she's actually visiting single.php.) If you change the index.php file to alter the way posts are displayed, you need to make the same changes in the single.php file. (You can make the same changes in both files, but WordPress doesn't automatically apply the changes from one file to the other.)

- **sidebar.php.** A blog without a sidebar is hardly a blog at all—at least, that's the way it feels these days. The sidebar has become an essential part of every blog, used to display anything from the proprietor's bio to a blogroll to pictures. The sidebar.php file is responsible for how the sidebar looks.

- **comments.php.** This file determines how comments are displayed for a post and what the comment form looks like. If you want to change any of the form labels, this file is the place to do it.

- **404.php.** A 404 error occurs when you point your browser to a page that no longer exists (or didn't exist to begin with). When the browser asks a Web server for something that doesn't exist, the server has nothing to show, so it returns a 404 error message. The 404.php file is a custom 404 error that you can make a little more useful with some tweaking. Instead of just saying that the page doesn't exist, you could serve up a search page so that your visitor can look for an answer instead of navigating away in frustration.

- **screenshot.png.** After you install a theme, a helpful screen shot appears in the Manage Themes screen (refer to Figure 12.1) to give you a sense of what the theme looks like. The screenshot.png file is the image that WordPress displays there. If a screen shot doesn't show up for a newly installed theme, make sure that the theme's folder contains a file with this name.

- **functions.php.** *Functions* are pieces of code that do particular tasks. Programmers place a bunch of these functions in a central place so that other parts of their code can access them. In WordPress, some themes have their own functions that are contained in the functions. php file. Looking at this file is fine, but unless you know a thing or two about PHP, I suggest that you leave it alone (or at least make a backup of the file before you change it).

Editing the theme with the Theme Editor

Because this book is about WordPress (in case you haven't noticed by now), you may as well use the built-in tool.

Working with the Theme Editor

To open the Theme Editor, click the Theme Editor link in the Appearance module of the navigation bar. You see a list of your theme's files on the right side of the resulting Edit Themes screen; the scrolling pane on the left side of the window displays the code of the selected file (**Figure 12.40**).

Figure 12.40 The Theme Editor.

The Theme Editor is a glorified text editor that's embedded in the Manage Themes screen, which means that you need an Internet connection to use it, like anything else in the WordPress administrative interface. Just select the file you want to edit in the list on the right side of the window, or choose it from the Select Theme to Edit drop-down menu. Either way, the file loads in the Theme Editor.

Viewing and editing the theme's code

note Because you're changing the actual files that make up the theme, be sure to back up your customized theme before you make any sort of change. Your changes aren't stored in a WordPress database but in the files themselves, so when you upload a new version of the directory to your Web host, you'll overwrite your custom copy unless you plan ahead.

The next step is looking for the code you want to change.

Suppose that you want to add a copyright date to the footer of your blog, which uses the default theme. Twenty Ten actually has a sidebar in the footer, so you could add a Text widget and be done with it, but for the sake of this example, you'll actually edit the code.

As you can see, my blog's footer has a link to my blog and a link to the WordPress site but no copyright date in sight (**Figure 12.41**). The footer information is contained in a file called footer.php.

Figure 12.41 A plain-vanilla Twenty Ten footer. No copyright notice means that people will feel free to steal my content!

Just select the footer.php file in the Theme Editor window. You'll see a bunch of code displayed on the left side. You're looking for this bit of code:

```
<div id="site-info">
        <a href="<?php echo home_url( '/' ) ?>" title="<?php
        ¬echo esc_attr( get_bloginfo( 'name', 'display' ) );
        ¬?>" rel="home">
        <?php bloginfo( 'name' ); ?>
 </a>
 </div><!-- #site-info -->
```

As you can see, this code constructs the link to your site dynamically, based on what you entered in your blog's settings. This means if you change the name of your blog, the footer link will update automatically, which is pretty neat.

To add a copyright notice after the link back to your blog, just add the bolded code below (feel free to use your own wording):

```
<div id="site-info">
 <a href="<?php echo home_url( '/' ) ?>" title="<?php echo
 ¬esc_attr( get_bloginfo( 'name', 'display' ) ); ?>" rel="home">
        <?php bloginfo( 'name' ); ?>
        </a> Everything Copyright me 2010
</div><!-- #site-info -->
```

Click the Update File button, and when you visit your blog again, the footer should have a copyright notice (**Figure 12.42**).

iPad Bungalow Everything Copyright me 2010   ⓦ *Proudly powered by WordPress.*

Figure 12.42 Ah—a simple bit of text completely protects my blog from naughty content thieves.

Granted, this example is a very simple one, but it got your feet wet with the Theme Editor. Chapter 13 delves further into this topic.

Keep in mind that most minor changes require some basic HTML knowledge, but you should feel comfortable poking around in any of the files that make up a theme. Just be sure to back up any files you plan to change so that you can recover quickly from any mistakes.

13

Theme Tweaking

Lots of people around the world use WordPress and love making themes for it. Best of all, lots of those fine folks want to share their themes with everyone, for free. Thanks to this virtual cornucopia of themes, chances are that you can find a WordPress theme that matches what you want your blog to look like. But what if you want to change something about a stock theme to make it a little closer to perfection (at least, to your idea of perfection)?

In this chapter, I give you the lowdown on customizing a stock theme to make it your own. This chapter won't teach you how to create a theme from scratch, but it'll give you enough know-how to tinker with existing themes.

Using the Theme Editor

Themes are just collections of PHP files, called *templates,* that perform different functions. You can edit theme files in your favorite text editor or use the WordPress Theme Editor, as I describe in this section.

note Before you edit any theme, be sure to back up its files. Theme files are located in *wordpress/*themes (where *wordpress* is your WordPress directory). Look for the directory named after the theme you're editing, and save a copy of that folder. Thereafter, if you mess up and want to revert to the original files, you'll have them right there.

To select a theme for editing in the Theme Editor, follow these steps:

1. Click the Appearance module in the admin navigation bar and then click the Editor link that appears.

    The Edit Themes page opens (**Figure 13.1**). The currently applied theme's templates are shown on the right side of the page, in the section called Templates. The Templates section of the Theme Editor lists a descriptive name for each file, and below it is the file name itself (Main Index Template and index.php, for example).

2. If you're interested in editing a theme other than the current one, choose it from the Select Theme to Edit drop-down menu and click the Select button.

3. Select the theme that you want to edit.

    All the templates that make up the selected theme load on the right side of the Theme Editor.

    After you've pointed the Theme Editor to the correct theme, it's time to select a template to edit.

Figure 13.1 The Theme Editor lets you edit themes as much as you like right inside WordPress.

4. Click the template you want to edit.

That template's descriptive name turns red with a blue background (**Figure 13.2**), and the Theme Editor displays the contents of the file—the code that runs your blog—in the pane on the left side of the page.

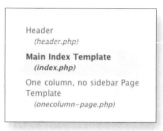

Figure 13.2 The template you selected is highlighted.

Some template files use *functions*—little computer programs written to do one thing that might apply to a wide range of templates. Functions help reduce the amount of code in a theme, because you don't have to keep repeating the same code over and over; you just write it and then call it in the template.

Whenever you're editing a template that includes functions, the Documentation drop-down menu appears below the file-editing window (**Figure 13.3**), listing all the functions in the file. You can check out that function's documentation by choosing it from the menu and clicking the Lookup button. The documentation for that function loads in a new browser window.

Figure 13.3 The Documentation drop-down menu lists all the functions in the selected template.

Tweaking a Stock Theme

Creating your own theme from scratch is beyond what 98 percent of WordPress users will ever need to do, which is why I recommend just finding a stock theme that you like. The idea is to take a theme and change certain parts of it—add a field here, take something away there—to make it your very own.

In this section, I show you how to change a few features of the default WordPress theme to make it more your own by altering the templates that make up the theme. In Chapter 9, I show you how to create a custom post type of book, and if you've been following along, you'll have noticed that posts with custom post types don't show up on the front page of the Twenty Ten theme. This section shows you how to display any custom post type on the front page of your blog.

Getting into The Loop

Before you dive headfirst into the theme's code, you need to understand a little bit about the workings of template code, which powers every WordPress theme.

WordPress templates use template tags for most of their functionality. These tags are much like HTML tags, with which you may be familiar, but they're a lot more powerful. Essentially, a *template tag* is a placeholder for some piece of information, such as the name of your blog, that you want to show up somewhere in your template. The name of your blog is something that you set, and WordPress stores that information in its database. The template tag `bloginfo()` is what you would use to return your blog's name, and in that case, it would look like this:

```
bloginfo('name'))
```

Template tags are the basis for all WordPress templates, and when they're combined with The Loop, they're very powerful. The most critical part of any theme, *The Loop* is a piece of code that powers much of WordPress.

To view The Loop, select the Twenty Ten theme in the Edit Themes page (see "Using the Theme Editor" earlier in this chapter), and select the loop.php file in the Templates section.

have_posts

The Twenty Ten theme uses The Loop in an advanced way, so don't be frightened by all the code you see. The first section of code is actually a little bit of documentation that tells you how the loop.php file works.

Scroll down in the editor until you see this code:

```php
<?php while ( have_posts() ) : the_post(); ?>
```

This line is the beginning of The Loop, which loops through all the content of your blog, specifying what content is displayed on the front page of your blog and how that content appears.

The first part, `<?php`, is just standard PHP code that isn't specific to WordPress. The `(have_posts() )` part is a function that queries your WordPress database to see whether you have any posts. If you do, it starts a `while` loop that iterates through each of your posts. Code is executed for each post in The Loop via several template tags, some of which work only within The Loop.

By default, the only post types that are included in The Loop are posts—that is, only blog posts are displayed on the front page of your blog. For this exercise, you want to include your custom post type book (see Chapter 9) on the front page. To have The Loop include both the post and book post types, you have to insert a line of code before The Loop starts so that it looks like this:

```php
<?php query_posts( array( 'post_type' =>
¬array('book', 'post') ) ); ?>
<?php while ( have_posts() ) : the_post(); ?>
```

By default, the query that gathers all the content to be used by The Loop includes only `'post'`. Adding the name of a custom post type—in this case, `'book'`—tells WordPress to include book post types on the front page of the blog.

title

Included in loop.php is the code that builds the titles of your posts. As I note earlier in this chapter, loop.php includes some logic for different sections of The Loop. To get to the code that determines the title format for posts (and any custom post types), scroll down until you see this comment in the code:

```php
<?php /* How to display all other posts. */ ?>
```

Everything after this comment affects how posts, and posts with custom post types, are displayed, as follows:

```
<h2 class="entry-title"><a href="<?php the_permalink();
¬?>" title="<?php printf( esc_attr__( 'Permalink to %s',
¬'twentyten' ), the_title_attribute( 'echo=0' ) ); ?>"
¬rel="bookmark"><?php the_title(); ?></a></h2>
```

All the WordPress magic happens between a pair of <h2> tags that make the title stand out. The tag called **the_permalink** returns the permalink of the post. This tag is used in conjunction with **the_title_attribute** (which returns a clean version of the title by stripping out any HTML code that may be used in the title) and **the_title** (which returns the title of the post as it was entered) to create the title link. If you want to add *Title:* before each of your blog post titles, the code would look like this:

```
<h2 class="entry-title">Title: <a href="<?php the_permalink();
¬?>" title="<?php printf( esc_attr__( 'Permalink to %s',
¬'twentyten' ), the_title_attribute( 'echo=0' ) ); ?>"
¬rel="bookmark"><?php the_title(); ?></a></h2>
```

Save the loop.php file by clicking the Update File button in the Edit Themes page, and reload your blog's home page, and you'll see *Title:* in each post's title (**Figure 13.4**). If you click the permalink and go to the post's page, however, you'll notice that *Title:* is missing. The reason: Individual post pages use a different template file (single.php).

Figure 13.4 The first fruits of theme tweaking: an addition to a post title. Useless? Perhaps, but the exercise is instructive.

note If you want the changes you've made in the loop.php file to show up on individual post pages, you have to edit that template separately. The single.php file uses the same tags as loop.php, so editing it should be a piece of cake.

Displaying the time

Below the title of your blog post, by default, WordPress displays the date when the post was published and its author. Suppose that you want to include the time when the post was published right next to the date, so that the line would read something like *Posted on October 2, 2011 at 11:19 pm*.

Twenty Ten uses a custom function called `twentyten_posted_on()` to generate this content. To edit that function, you need to switch the Theme Editor to display the file called Theme Functions by selecting it in the Templates list on the right side of the Theme Editor (refer to Figure 13.1). This file contains all the custom functions that Twenty Ten uses.

The file is rather lengthy, so I suggest using your browser's find function to located the `twentyten_posted_on()` code, which looks like this:

```
function twentyten_posted_on() {
    printf( __( '<span class="%1$s">Posted on</span> %2$s
    ¬<span class="meta-sep">by</span> %3$s', 'twentyten' ),
            'meta-prep meta-prep-author',
            sprintf( '<a href="%1$s" title="%2$s"
            ¬rel="bookmark"><span class="entry-date">
            ¬%3$s</span></a>',
                get_permalink(),
                esc_attr( get_the_time() ),
                get_the_date()
        ),
            sprintf( '<span class="author vcard">
            ¬<a class="url fn n" href="%1$s"
            ¬title="%2$s">%3$s</a></span>',
            get_author_posts_url( get_the_author_meta
            ¬( 'ID' ) ),
                sprintf( esc_attr__( 'View all posts by
                ¬%s', 'twentyten' ), get_the_author() ),
```

```
                                get_the_author()
                        )
                );
        }
endif;
```

That mess of code produces the header information for all your posts. The part that you're interested in at the moment is this part:

```
sprintf( '<a href="%1$s" title="%2$s" rel="bookmark">
¬<span class="entry-date">%3$s</span></a>',
                                get_permalink(),
                                esc_attr( get_the_time() ),
                                get_the_date()
                ),
```

That code is responsible for displaying a time stamp below the post type. First, `sprintf` takes some inputs (like WordPress functions) and returns text (called a *string* by programmers) that WordPress can display. The first half of the function (everything between the quotes) determines how the information provided by the inputs—the list of three functions in the second half (`get_permalink()`, `get_the_time()`, and `get_the_date()`)—are used to create the text you see on the blog.

> **note** `get_permalink()`, `get_the_time()`, and `get_the_date()` are special WordPress functions that work only when they're used within The Loop. If you try to use them somewhere in a template outside The Loop, you'll get an error.

Here's another programming term for you: *variables,* which are placeholders whose value is set by something else. The preceding block of code has three variables: `%1$s`, `%2$s`, and `%3$s`. Each of these variables has its values set by one of the three functions in the second half of the `sprintf` function:

- `get_permalink()` returns the permalink of the current post.
- `get_the_time()` returns the time when the current post was published.
- `get_the_date()` returns the date on which the current post was published.

Because you're after adding the time to the display, you know that you need to use %2$s to place it. Changing the code as follows is all it takes:

```
sprintf( '<a href="%1$s" title="%2$s" rel="bookmark">
¬<span class="entry-date">%3$s</span></a> at %2$s',
                        get_permalink(),
                        esc_attr( get_the_time() ),
                        get_the_date()
    )
```

Now the time is displayed right below the title of the post (**Figure 13.5**).

Blogging on the iPad

Posted on October 2, 2010 at 11:29 pm by scott

Figure 13.5 Just like that, you have the time displayed for all to see.

Just the Beginning

Adding the time to your post's header is just the tip of the iceberg when it comes to customizing WordPress themes. You can change just about everything, if you have the gumption and the knowledge.

I can't give you gumption, but I can point you toward some documentation that can answer all your questions about template tags—the building blocks of WordPress themes. Check out the WordPress Codex's Template Tags page at http://codex.wordpress.org/Template_Tags to find out more about all the great things you can do with tags.

14

Using Plug-Ins

Plug-ins extend what WordPress can do by adding new functionality and features with minimal effort on your part. A dizzying array of plug-ins, both paid and free, is available for WordPress. In fact, for many people, this extensive selection of plug-ins is why they choose WordPress over other blogging tools.

What the heck is a *plug-in?* It's a file (or several files, depending on how complicated the plug-in is) that you upload to your blog.

To see the default plug-ins in your WordPress installation, click the Plugins link in the navigation bar of the WordPress administration interface (**Figure 14.1** on the next page). WordPress opens the Plugins screen (**Figure 14.2** on the next page), which displays the currently installed plug-ins. An *installed plug-in* is one that you've uploaded and saved in *wordpress/*wp-content/plugins (where *wordpress* is your WordPress installation folder) either manually or by using WordPress to install it (more on this in a moment).

Figure 14.1 The Plugins module in the WordPress navigation bar.

Figure 14.2 The Plugins screen looks like the long-lost cousin of the Pages and Posts screens.

In WordPress, two plug-ins are installed by default: Akismet and something called Hello Dolly (hello.php). Just having them installed isn't enough, though. To use a plug-in, you have to activate it—as I show you in this chapter.

Managing Plug-Ins

Managing plug-ins begins with seeing which plug-ins are active and which are inactive. In a fresh WordPress installation, you have only inactive plug-ins, which you can see by clicking the All link or the Inactive link at the top of the Plugins screen (refer to Figure 14.2). Inactive plug-ins are displayed with a gray background so you can see them at a glance.

WordPress displays information about these plug-ins in two columns:

- **Plugin.** The Plugin column lists plug-ins in alphabetical order by name.

- **Description.** The Description column tells you what the plug-in does and who wrote it. It also includes, directly below the text of the description, the version number, the creator, and a link to the plug-in's Web site.

    Hello Dolly, for example, doesn't do anything especially useful, but having a line from the musical *Hello, Dolly* displayed on your admin pages can't be a bad thing. (I may be biased, though: I grew up in Yonkers, New York, where most of the action in *Hello, Dolly* takes place.)

Right below the name of each plug-in, you'll notice some links. These are the actions you can perform on each plug-in, such as Activate (inactive plug-ins only), Deactivate (active plug-ins only), Edit, or Delete (inactive plug-ins only).

Activating a plug-in

To use a plug-in, you have to activate it. You can accomplish this task in either of two ways in the Plugins screen:

- Click the check box of the plug-in you want to activate (or select multiple check boxes to activate multiple plug-ins at the same time), choose Activate from the Bulk Actions drop-down menu, and click the Apply button next to that menu.

- Click the Activate link below the name of the plug-in.

This method works on only one plug-in at a time.

No matter which method you use, WordPress displays a little notice that your plug-in has been activated. It also displays a new Active section in the Plugins screen (**Figure 14.3** on the next page). This new section is displayed first at the top of the screen now, followed by the Inactive section. Also, active plug-ins are displayed with a white background, which makes it easier to tell at a glance which plug-ins are active.

Figure 14.3 Hello Dolly is activated.

Several things may happen after you activate a plug-in. Hello Dolly is simple and doesn't add any menu items; all it does is display a lyric from the musical on your admin pages (**Figure 14.4**). The Akismet plug-in, on the other hand, adds a menu item to the Plugins screen; I cover it in detail in Chapter 11.

Figure 14.4 These words in the top-right corner of this admin page are lyrics from *Hello, Dolly.* The plug-in works!

Editing a plug-in

Like WordPress itself, plug-ins consist of files—text files, in this case, which you can edit. You can access the editing tools in either of two ways:

- Click the Edit link below the plug-in's name (refer to "Managing Plug-Ins" earlier in this chapter).

- Click the Editor link in the Plugins module in the navigation bar (refer to Figure 14.1).

Either action opens the Plugin Editor's Edit Plugins screen (**Figure 14.5**). Much like the Theme Editor's Edit Themes screen (which I cover in Chapter 12), this screen allows you to edit the files that make up your installed plug-ins.

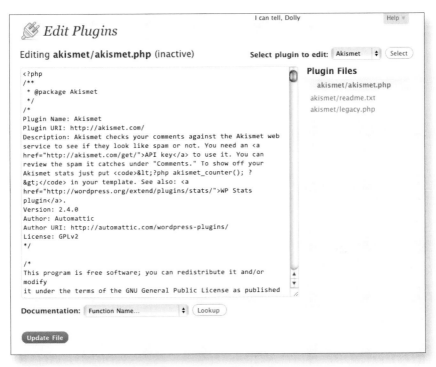

Figure 14.5 The Plugin Editor allows you to edit plug-ins.

The scrolling pane on the left side of the screen displays the code of the file that's selected on the right side of the screen. If you've loaded the Plugin Editor by clicking the Edit link below a particular plug-in's name in the Plugins screen (refer to Figure 14.2), the Plugin Editor loads that file. The header gives you some information about the file you're editing, including its directory, its name, and its status (active or inactive).

The right side of the screen lists all the plug-in files that are available for editing. Click the name of a plug-in to load its code into the pane on the left side of the screen. You can simply look at the code and read the comments or change anything you want. Much as you can in the Theme Editor, you need more information on anything in the code, you can use the Documentation drop-down menu to look it up. (See Chapter 13 for details.)

If you make any edits—and before you do, be sure that you know what you're doing!—click the Update File button to save your changes.

Be careful while editing a plug-in. Changing or deleting code can have unintended consequences, even though reinstalling a plug-in is fairly easy.

Updating a plug-in

Just like all other software developers, plug-in authors continually change and update their products. Keeping your plug-ins up to date used to be a manual process, but nowadays, WordPress keeps track of your plug-ins and alerts you when updates are available. A small speech-bubble number appears next to the Plugins item in the admin navigation bar (much like when you have new comments), and an Upgrade Available link appears at the top of the Plugins screen when updates are available (**Figure 14.6**).

Figure 14.6 WordPress alerts you that three plug-ins need updates.

Click the link to see information about the update(s) (**Figure 14.7**).

Figure 14.7 Details about an Akismet update.

 Pay attention to what versions of WordPress a plug-in supports, especially when a new version of WordPress is released. Sometimes, plug-ins need to be updated to play nicely with WordPress changes.

WordPress gives you two options for updating a plug-in:

- Click the View Version x.x Details link to download the new version of the plug-in and install it at your leisure.

- Click the Upgrade Automatically link to download the update, decompress it, remove the old plug-in, and install the new one.

> **note**
>
> **You may not want to use the automatic-upgrade method if you want to check out the new features of a plug-in update before you install it.**

Deactivating a plug-in

If you can activate a plug-in, it stands to reason that you can deactivate it as well. Deactivating a plug-in doesn't uninstall it; rather, deactivating it tells WordPress not to load the plug-in's extensions. The features of a deactivated plug-in are no longer accessible via the administration interface.

You have two ways to deactivate a plug-in:

- In the Active section of the Plugins screen (refer to Figure 14.3), click the check box of the plug-in you want to deactivate (or click multiple check boxes to deactivate multiple plug-ins at the same time); then choose Deactivate from the Bulk Actions drop-down menu, and click the Apply button next to that menu.

- Click the Deactivate link below the name of the plug-in you're no longer interested in running.

> **note**
>
> **This method works on only one plug-in at a time.**

When you deactivate a plug-in, another new section appears at the top of the Plugins screen: Recently Active (**Figure 14.8**).

Figure 14.8 The Recently Active section.

A deactivated plug-in is listed in this section for seven days before it returns to the Inactive section, so you can see what plug-ins you used recently and reactivate them if you want (using the methods in "Activating a plug-in" earlier in this chapter). If you want to clear this display, click the Clear List button; all the plug-ins listed in the Recently Active section immediately move to the Inactive section.

Deleting a plug-in

Plug-ins are so easy to install, I'm willing to bet that you'll soon have a large number of them cluttering your blog. Sure, you can deactivate plug-ins when you're done with them, but what if you decide that you don't want a certain plug-in installed in your blog at all?

Deleting a plug-in is just as easy as installing one, and you can do it in either of two ways. I describe both methods in the following sections.

Using the Plugins screen

In either the Inactive or Recently Active section of the Plugins screen, check the check boxes of the plug-ins that you want to delete; then choose Delete from the Bulk Actions drop-down menu, and click the Apply button. WordPress displays the Delete Plugin(s) dialog box (**Figure 14.9**).

Figure 14.9 WordPress knows that people sometimes click Delete by accident, so it asks you to confirm your action.

WordPress wants to make sure that you really want to delete the plug-in, because no undo option is available. You can see all the files associated with this plug-in by clicking the link titled Click to View Entire List of Files Which Will Be Deleted.

When you're sure what you want to do, click Yes, Delete These Files to delete the plug-in, or click No, Return Me to the Plugin List if you have a last-minute change of heart.

Using an FTP program

If you prefer, you can use your FTP program of choice to navigate to the wp-content/plugins directory and delete the folder containing the files for the plug-in you want to remove. The beauty of this method is that it works even when WordPress isn't able to delete the plug-in for some reason.

Finding Plug-Ins

Clicking the Add New button at the top of the Plugins screen (refer to Figure 14.2) takes you to a specialized search screen, embedded right there in your blog's admin screen, for the official WordPress Plugin Directory (http://wordpress.org/extend/plugins). This screen (**Figure 14.10**) is your one-stop shop for all WordPress-related plug-ins—well, most of them, anyway.

Figure 14.10   The Plugin Directory within WordPress itself.

The screen has six sections (though I'm going to group the last three together):

- **Search.** This section allows you to search the Plugin Directory or use the links in the Popular Tags pane to find plug-ins tagged with those terms.

- **Upload.** You can upload your own plug-ins directly to your WordPress installation here.

- **Featured.** This section lists plug-ins that the staff of the Plugin Directory deem worthy of your attention. Check 'em out!

- **Popular, Newest,** and **Recently Updated.** These three sections list plug-ins that belong to each of these categories.

You can also search for a particular plug-in by name or by a subject if you want your WordPress blog to do something but aren't sure whether a plug-in is available to handle the job.

Each plug-in entry lists the plug-in's name and version number; a rating; and a description, which mentions the author of the plug-in (**Figure 14.11**).

Two links appear below the name of the plug-in: Details, which is a link to a page that provides more details about the plug-in, and Install Now, which installs the plug-in.

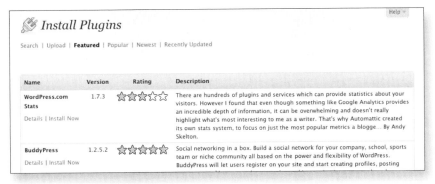

Figure 14.11 A list of featured plug-ins.

Clicking the Details link below a plug-in's name reveals a more in-depth description of that plug-in (**Figure 14.12**). In the right column, below the red Install Now button, you see the version number, the author, when the plug-in was last updated, which versions of WordPress are supported, and how many times the plug-in has been downloaded.

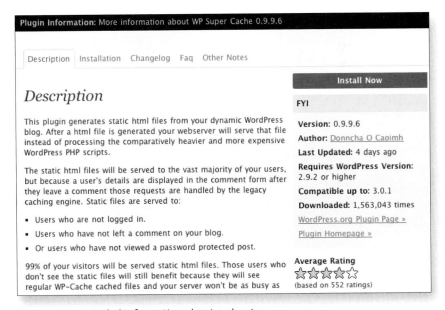

Figure 14.12 Detailed information about a plug-in.

A few tabs run along the top of this window. Description is selected by default; you can switch to Installation (notes about installing the plug-in), Changelog (a list of what features changed in various versions of the plug-in), Faq (frequently asked questions), and Other Notes. Clicking a tab reveals its contents.

 note **Pay close attention to the version of WordPress that the plug-in requires and what it's compatible with. If the version of WordPress you're running falls outside those boundaries, you shouldn't install the plug-in.**

Creating a Plug-In of Your Very Own

Plug-ins can get pretty complicated, requiring knowledge of PHP that goes beyond the scope of this book. But if you want to create your own plug-ins, you should be aware of a formatting issue: If you want your custom plug-in's name, version number, and description to show up in the Plugins screen, you need to include some important header information in a PHP comment. (PHP comments start with /* and end with */.)

Here's an example plug-in that does nothing other than show up correctly in the Plugins screen:

```
<?php
/*
Plugin Name: My totally awesome plug-in
Plugin URI: http://www.wordpressforall.com/
Description: This plug-in is only for demonstration purposes
¬related to the blog <a href=
¬"http://www.wordpressforall.com/">WordPress For All</a>.
Author: Scott McNulty
Author URI: http://blog.blankbaby.com/
Version: 1.0
*/

?>
```

Plug-ins are written in PHP, which means that you have to open the <php> tag first to let the server know how to handle this file. The rest of the code provides WordPress information to display in the Plugins screen. Here's a breakdown of the elements of this code:

- **Plugin Name.** This variable sets the display name of the plug-in— in this case, *My totally awesome plug-in.* That name will be displayed in the Name column of each plug-in table.

> **note**   **The names of the files that make up your plug-ins don't matter to WordPress, so you can name them whatever you like, but the best practice is to follow a naming convention of some kind.**

- **Plugin URI.** This variable is a Web site that contains more information about your plug-in. The name of your plug-in is a link to this site.

- **Description.** This variable describes your plug-in. Make sure that the description gives people who download your plug-in a good idea of what the plug-in actually does. You can use HTML in this description, so you can link to Web sites that may give the user more information.

- **Author.** You should get credit for all your hard plug-in coding, right? Good thing you do! Simply add your name to this section of the header, and WordPress will credit the plug-in to you.

- **Author URI.** This variable is a link to your Web site, using the Author entry as the text of the link.

- **Version.** For this variable, enter the version number of your plug-in.

Close the comments and then enter the PHP code that makes your plug-in do something. (This example plug-in doesn't do anything.) Finally, close the PHP tag. **Figure 14.13** shows the result.

Figure 14.13 This demonstration plug-in doesn't do anything other than set the proper information for display.

Plug-Ins No Blog Should Be Without

Countless plug-ins are available for WordPress, and all those choices can be a little overwhelming. I'm going to give you a list of four plug-ins that I install in every WordPress blog that I run. I'm not associated with the developers of these plug-ins, all of which are free (though many of the developers accept donations). I just find these plug-ins to be the best of breed, and I can't imagine using WordPress without them.

Here are my top four WordPress plug-ins, in no particular order:

All in One SEO Pack

http://wordpress.org/extend/plugins/ all-in-one-seo-pack

SEO stands for *search engine optimization,* which basically answers the question "How do I get my blog to show up first on Google?" All in One SEO Pack gives you a lot of options and post/page settings that allow you to make your blog a search-engine darling. Be sure to read the documentation for this plug-in; it's very powerful.

podPress

http://wordpress.org/extend/plugins/podpress

If you plan on having a podcast, you need to get podPress. This great plug-in makes podcasting ridiculously easy, embedding the media files for you, helping you get your podcast into podcasting directories, and generally making your life as a podcaster much smoother. A premium (read: paid) version adds some features, but most people will be happy with the free version.

Exploit Scanner

http://wordpress.org/extend/plugins/exploit-scanner

The Internet can be a scary place, and because so many people use WordPress, it's an attractive target for hackers. Exploit Scanner is a simple plug-in that scans your installation and looks for anything out of the ordinary. Those odd things may mean that your blog has been hacked, which is never fun. Exploit Scanner will tell you what is hacked and how to fix it.

Bad Behavior

http://wordpress.org/extend/plugins/bad-behavior

Akismet (see Chapter 11) fights comment spam by cataloging various identifying marks and then sending comments that have those marks to the spam queue. Bad Behavior stops the bots that leave comment spam from leaving the spam in the first place

15

Troubleshooting and Maintenance

I've been running WordPress blogs for a long time, and I haven't run into many major issues over the years. This fact speaks to the hard work that faceless coding volunteers do to make WordPress as solid a product as it is. Still, you should know some things to check in the unlikely event that you run into an issue. You can also save yourself a heaping helping of grief by doing some small things to make sure that your copy of WordPress stays a lean, mean blogging machine.

Troubleshooting Problems

Problems always crop up, but all is not lost when you encounter a problem. Don't panic. In this section, I outline a few simple troubleshooting steps that should get you out of many common jams.

You get an error instead of blog content

The most common issue that you'll encounter in WordPress is trouble with the communications between your installation of WordPress and the database that holds your blog's users, content, and some settings. **Figure 15.1** shows one example: the dreaded "Error establishing a database connection" error.

Figure 15.1 An error message alerting you that something's amiss with your database.

If you see an error like this one, your blog can't talk to its database. You can try the following steps in order:

1. Make sure that your database server is up.

If your database server is down, you can do little to fix this error other than get the database server back online. WordPress is highly dynamic, meaning that it queries the database to build all pages (both public and admin pages), so without a database, WordPress is fairly useless.

note   **You may have to call your Web-hosting company to ask whether this server is down.**

2. Try connecting to your database with whatever management tools you use.

    If the database is up and running, the problem is with WordPress.

3. Check your wp-config.php file to make sure that the DB_NAME, DB_USER, DB_PASSWORD, and DB_HOST parameters all have the proper information.

    See Chapter 2 for details on editing your wp-config file.

> **tip**   **Whenever you change the database's user password (for security reasons or what have you), make sure that you update the wp-config file with the proper values.**

    If the wp-config file shows that all your database information is correct, you should try one last step:

4. Reset the WordPress database's user password in both the wp-config file and MySQL.

    This step ensures that both passwords are the same and should fix the problem. See Chapter 2 for more information.

You can't log in to WordPress

If you have this problem, chances are that you've just forgotten your password. (It happens to the best of us.)

To solve the problem, follow these steps:

1. Click the Lost Your Password? link below the login form.

    WordPress takes you to the Get New Password window (**Figure 15.2**).

Figure 15.2 Enter your user name or email address in this window.

2. Enter your user name or your email address in the text box.

note The email address you enter has to be the one associated with your WordPress account (see Chapter 2).

3. Click the Get New Password button.

WordPress sends an email message to the address you entered in Step 2.

4. Click the link in this e-mail message (**Figure 15.3**) to generate a new password for your account.

WordPress sends the new password to you.

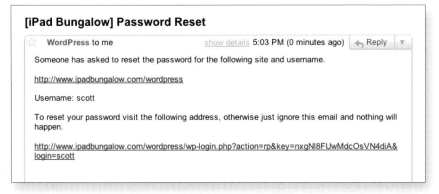

[iPad Bungalow] Password Reset

WordPress to me   show details 5:03 PM (0 minutes ago)   Reply   ▼

Someone has asked to reset the password for the following site and username.

http://www.ipadbungalow.com/wordpress

Username: scott

To reset your password visit the following address, otherwise just ignore this email and nothing will happen.

http://www.ipadbungalow.com/wordpress/wp-login.php?action=rp&key=nxgNI8FUwMdcOsVN4diA&login=scott

Figure 15.3   The email contains a link that allows you to reset your password.

note If you don't click the link in the email message, your password isn't reset. This feature safeguards against someone locking you out of your own blog by changing your password.

tip If you generate a random password, be sure to change your password to something more memorable after you log in. See Chapter 3 for details.

Your blog has been hacked! OMG!

One downfall of using the most popular blogging software out there is that WordPress blogs are targets for hackers. If you don't keep your WordPress installation current (see "WordPress updates are also your friends" later in this chapter), someone could exploit a known security vulnerability in your blog. I've seen this situation happen to very savvy bloggers (including my wife!), so don't think that it can't happen to you.

Generally, a hacker crafts a bot that trawls the Internet looking for vulnerable installations of WordPress. When it finds a vulnerable blog, the bot exploits the vulnerability to access your blog and insert links to various sites of ill repute. This technique is an effort to use your blog to increase those sites' Google PageRank scores.

 note **PageRank is an algorithm that Google uses to assign scores to all pages in its index. The higher the score, the better, so getting more links increases a site's PageRank score.**

Chances are that if you see several odd links on your blog, you've been hacked. To regain control, follow these steps:

1. Calm down.

    Having your blog hacked sucks, but you could suffer far worse cyber-crimes. (Identity theft tops the list in my book.)

2. Let your Web host know.

    Giving your host notice alerts the company to check its systems (and its other customers' servers).

3. Change your WordPress password, your Web-hosting account password, and the FTP password associated with your Web-hosting account.

tip **You shouldn't use the same user name/password combo for your blog that you do for all your other online accounts.**

4. Check out the Users page in WordPress, and delete any users that you didn't create—especially any that have Administrator privileges.

    Chapter 3 has all the details on managing users, including the Users page.

5. Log in to your database, using your database management tool of choice; double-check all the users there; and delete any users that you didn't create.

6. Change the database user password, and update the wp-config file (refer to "You get an error instead of blog content" earlier in this chapter).

7. Delete your themes (which have most likely been hacked to display those spam links), and reinstall them.

   Turn to Chapter 12 for directions on installing themes.

8. If you've been very good about backing up your data, completely delete and then reinstall WordPress (see Chapter 2).

   This method is the only way to make sure that all remnants of the hack are erased.

Heading off Trouble Before It Begins

Troubleshooting means that you're in trouble. I'd much rather avoid trouble and get on with the rest of my life (in which I avoid all sorts of other work; it's a skill). You can do a few simple things to keep your WordPress blog in tip-top shape and avoid trouble in the long run.

Backups are your friends

One plug-in that didn't make my list in Chapter 14, but that's still worth a look, is WP-DB-Backup (http://wordpress.org/extend/plugins/wp-db-backup), which backs up your MySQL data automatically. You don't have to do anything (win!). Making backups of your database covers your users and content, but it doesn't cover anything that's in your wp-content folder (see Chapter 2). You'll have to back up your Media Library, plug-ins, and themes separately.

If you don't mind spending a little money, and you want to make your backups complete and worry-free, you should check into VaultPress (www.vaultpress.com). This backup service is run by Automattic, the company behind WordPress. Pricing starts at $20 a month per blog, which isn't that much if your blog is a very important part of your life.

note   At the time I'm writing this chapter, VaultPress isn't open to the public. You can apply for a spot, though, and generally, you'll get in.

Using the Export screen

If you don't want to use a plug-in or need to make a one-off backup of the contents of your blog, choose Tools > Export to open the Export screen (**Figure 15.4**), where you can export some or all of your blog's content to an XML file.

Figure 15.4 The WordPress Export screen makes it a breeze to export your WordPress content to an XML file.

If you want to export all of your blog's content, just leave all the filters set to their default values and click the Download Export File button.

note   You can export only text from this screen; you still need to back up your files and wp-content folder separately.

Exporting posts by author

One of the nicest things about the WordPress export functionality is that you can choose to export only posts by one author. This feature comes in handy in a multiple-poster blog when one author decides that he wants to strike out on his own. You can give this person a file containing just his posts.

To export a single author's posts, follow these steps:

1. Choose Tools > Export.

   The Export screen opens.

2. From the Authors drop-down menu, choose the author you're interested in.

3. Click the Download Export File button.

   WordPress creates a file of the author's posts.

Importing export files

When you have an export file, you'll probably want to do something with it. To import export files into WordPress, follow these steps:

1. Choose Tools > Import to open the Import screen.

   This screen lists all the available import plug-ins.

2. Click the WordPress option to install the WordPress Import plug-in.

3. Activate the WordPress Import plug-in (see Chapter 14 for directions).

   The Import WordPress panel opens.

4. Select your file, and click the Choose button.

5. Click the Upload File and Import button.

   WordPress imports the content.

When you import from a WordPress backup, you have several options:

- You can map the authors in the file to existing authors in your WordPress blog, or you can have the authors in the import file created automatically in addition to the existing authors (**Figure 15.5**).

Figure 15.5 The Assign Authors page gives you several import options.

- You can have WordPress attempt to download files that are attached to the exported posts (assuming that those files are accessible from their original URLs).

WordPress updates are also your friends

WordPress updates often come at a fast and furious rate, and they can be tough to keep up with. But I strongly urge you to keep your blog as current as possible. Luckily, WordPress alerts you when a new update is available for download.

The point releases are especially important because they're released to address known flaws. (*Point release* is software speak for a release that doesn't add features but focuses on bug and security fixes. It increments the version number by only a point, so WordPress 3.0 becomes WordPress 3.0.1.)

tip Subscribe to the WordPress Development Updates blog
(http://wpdevel.wordpress.com) to keep abreast of WordPress
news such as updates.

WordPress makes keeping up to date very easy. When a new version of
WordPress is available, an alert is displayed in your blog's Dashboard
(**Figure 15.6**). Clicking the Please Update Now link takes you to the Update
screen, which is a central place for updating plug-ins, themes, and
WordPress itself.

Figure 15.6 WordPress wants you to stay up to date, so it will nag you in
the Dashboard.

You can choose to update WordPress automatically by clicking the Please
Update Now link, which takes you to the Update screen. There, you can click
Update Automatically, and WordPress will take care of the update for you, or
you can download the current version of WordPress and update your installation manually (which means backing up your wp-content folder and
wp-config.php file, and then installing the new WordPress files over the
old ones). Either way, your blog stays up to date, and you stay one step
ahead of the hackers.

The pain of popularity

WordPress generates pages dynamically as people load them. No page is
ever out of date; WordPress always displays the information as you have it
entered in your database. Update a post, and the very next person who
reads that post sees your changes. This feature is truly great.

Well, actually, it's great until a link to your blog gets posted to Digg. Then
thousands of people start loading your blog, generating tens of thousands
of queries against your database server to generate the same page for each
visitor. This sudden upswing in traffic brings down your database, and as
you know, WordPress can't display anything without a database. This situation is where the concept of caching comes into play.

Several WordPress plug-ins can help you weather a sudden influx of traffic without having to pony up the money for a beefier Web-hosting contract. Myself, I'm a fan of WP Super Cache (http://wordpress.org/extend/plugins/wp-super-cache).

Caching works on the simple concept that most of the content on your blog doesn't change much, so why create the pages from scratch every time someone visits? Instead, you can keep a premade copy on hand and serve that copy up to your visitors. This method lessens the impact on the database server, which doesn't need to provide all that information for every page, and it lessens the load on the Web server, which can serve up only static files that don't require processing.

You don't have to wait for your blog to become incredibly popular to install these caching options. Forewarned is forearmed. It's best to prepare your blog for heavy traffic, because you can't always predict what will catch the eyes of the Internet hordes.

note **The downside of caching is that if you update a page, it may take a little while for the change to be reflected on your site. Keep this drawback in mind if you update your blog frequently.**

16

Bloggerly Wisdom

Up to this point, I've shown you how to install, manage, and update a WordPress blog. This knowledge is critical to a successful blog, because otherwise, you wouldn't know what to do with a blog! A blog is much more than the software that runs behind the scenes, however. It's important to know about themes, widgets, and plug-ins, because you can use all those features to enhance your blog, but the true star of the show is your content, whether it be photos, videos, or words.

In this chapter, I give you some tips, tricks, and techniques for building an audience for your blog and show you how you should gauge success. My advice boils down to what I call the Three Cs of Blogging: Content, Consistency, and Community.

As you read this chapter, keep in mind how you define success. Not everyone blogs to gain a massive readership. Some people keep personal blogs that no one other than the person writing the blog reads, and they're very happy with that situation. If you blog just to keep your family up to date on your life, chances are that a publisher won't be calling you with a lucrative book deal based on that blog, but you'll be far better connected with your family.

Most of the advice in this chapter assumes that you want to grow your blog's readership, but you shouldn't feel any pressure to do that. Personally, I blog because blogging makes me happy. If other people happen to like what I'm sharing, that's cool, but that's not what keeps me blogging.

Content

Bill Gates—yes, that Bill Gates—once said, "Content is king." Putting aside any feelings you may have about the man, you've gotta admit he was on to something. Now more than ever, content rules the roost, even while media companies (and bloggers) are trying to figure out how to make a little moola from all that great content.

Bust the blogging myths

I've been lucky enough to be a professional blogger for several years, and in that time, I've heard a couple of myths about blog content over and over again.

Myth #1: Blog posts have to be short

I'm not sure how this myth entered into the conventional wisdom about blogging, but it just isn't true. There's no "magic" length for blog posts. Short blog posts work, as do long blog posts. Heck, throw in a medium-length blog post once in a while, and you'll find that people respond to it. A well-written blog post will be read regardless of its length.

Myth #2: Blogging doesn't require work

Because blogging is so casual, many people assume that you write something and then post it immediately. Some posts are like that, but writing a good blog post takes work.

How do you know whether a blog post is "good"? It's very difficult to predict what your readers will enjoy, but here are a couple of tips you can use to make sure that your writing won't undermine your ideas:

- **Proofread your posts.** Lots of bloggers feel that the relatively relaxed nature of blogging means that spelling and grammar can go out the window. After you write a post, no matter how long it is, walk away from it for 5 to 10 minutes; then come back to it, and check it over for flow and grammar. Don't forget to run a spell check too.

- **Read your posts out loud.** This tip is an old writer's trick. When you read (silently) something you've written, your mind has a funny habit of reading what you *meant* to write rather than the actual words on the page, so you may not notice omitted words or poor transitions. When you read something out loud, however, your ear picks up things that just don't sound right (and won't read right, either). Trust me—you'll be amazed how much your writing will improve when you do this.

Find a niche, and totally niche it up

One piece of advice that you'll hear from wizened bloggers is to pick a niche topic and really focus on it. Suppose that you're into technology. It seems to follow that you'll want to start your very own tech blog, from which you'll make millions of dollars, and then you'll finally be able to build that robot army you've always dreamed of.

Keep in mind, though, that your upstart tech blog will be competing with a lot of general tech blogs, many of which have large and established audiences. Why should they link to your blog, which covers the same subject that they cover?

This is where concentrating on one particular topic comes into play. If you focus on a specific topic and go for deep coverage, as opposed to broad coverage, your chances of gaining an audience improve. It's true that when you limit your subject—say, covering robot armies instead of general tech—you also limit your audience, and limiting your audience seems like the last thing you'd want to do. Right?

Maybe not. People who are interested in a super-specific topic are often *very* interested in said topic. If you're able to tap into that kind of interested audience, you're guaranteed a loyal fan base, small though it may be.

As you gain an audience (by leveraging the Three Cs of Blogging), you'll notice something: People will consider you to be an expert on robot armies. You'll be invited to participate in panels about robot armies at supervillain conventions, and other robot-army bloggers will be emailing you and following you on Twitter. Basically, you'll be a big fish in a small pond, and when you've gotten some blog cred, you can try to expand your blog's subject matter.

The Curse of the Niche

Niches give, and niches take away. Niche topics click with highly engaged audiences, which is great, but those audiences sometimes react poorly when you blog about something outside your niche, much as they do when a cast member from *Star Trek* (other than William Shatner) appears on another show. You're willing to give the actors the benefit of the doubt, mostly, but they'll always be Uhura and Chekov to you.

You gotta be you

When you come right down to it, the blogging system that you use matters very little to the success of your blog. Sure, you'll be more likely to post if you use a well-designed blogging tool like WordPress, which gets out of your way and helps you concentrate on blogging, but *you* are the key factor in your blog. Your passion, your knowledge, and your viewpoint will make your blog stand out from the rest.

Bloggers have a reputation for being an opinionated lot, and there's some truth to that rep. People don't want to hear about what happened to you during your day or about the news: They want to hear how you felt about those events. You need look no further than the cable news networks to know that a strong viewpoint is important in establishing a media presence, both online and off.

note	I caution you not to court controversy just for the sake of being controversial, though. This tactic may reap you short-term rewards, but you'll gain a reputation for that sort of thing if you continue to engage in it.

People like pictures

WordPress offers impressive support for embedding media in your posts (check out Chapter 6 for the lowdown on media), and for good reason: Nothing spruces up a blog post like a great picture that helps drive your point home.

Video on the Web is hip and hot. Everyone wants to include video in blogs (even this book has accompanying videos that you can purchase), and generally, I think video is a great way to share your passion with people.

If you're going to be working with video, keep in mind two things that can make or break a video:

- **Lighting.** Make sure that you're well illuminated; no one wants to watch a shadowy figure for any length of time. Sit near a window—but not in front of one, because you'll be backlighted, and no one will be able to see you—or film outside if at all possible. The sun is the best and most flattering light around.

- **Sound.** People need to be able to see you, but more important, they need to be able to hear what you're saying. They'll forgive you for bad lighting, but nothing makes them stop watching a video like a high-pitched hum or muffled voice. Invest in a good microphone for your camera, or get an external microphone if you can. It'll be worth the money.

Consistency

A few years ago, I was in charge of a rather large group blog devoted to covering the computer company Apple and all that goes along with it. Because I was in charge, I was tasked with increasing the blog's traffic, which is a reasonable thing to ask.

Taking a look at the visitor statistics, I noticed something interesting: On the days when more posts were written, traffic surged, and on days with few or no posts, traffic took a big dip. The reason seems pretty obvious—why would you expect to get lots of traffic on a day when you haven't posted anything?—but many people overlook it.

Get into the habit of posting on a regular schedule. The group blog I was running included more than ten other bloggers, so it was reasonable to have a schedule of adding a new post at the top of every hour on weekdays from 9 a.m. to 6 p.m. Any additional posts were scheduled to publish on the half-hour, and breaking news got posted without regard to the schedule.

I'm not suggesting that you need to post ten things a day on your blog, but if you want to develop an audience, you need to provide piping-hot content on a regular basis. Perhaps you can manage to put up a new post every other day or once a week. (If you're blogging just for fun, of course, you should feel free to post whenever you like.)

Keep an Editorial Calendar

All writers know the terror of staring at a blank piece of paper (or an empty Add New Post page). Inspiration is a fickle thing, and when you're trying to pump out prose on a schedule, you really can't wait for a lightning bolt from the heavens to strike, giving you a brilliant idea. You just have to fill that empty post form with some words.

An editorial calendar is your best weapon to combat writers' block. As you might guess, this calendar lists when you'll write about a certain subject. Setting up a structure lets you stop worrying about *what* you'll write and concentrate on *when* you'll write it. During the holidays, for example, it would make sense to plan a series of buying-guide posts, because people will be looking for cool things to buy as presents.

The best part of an editorial calendar is that you can work on it when you're inspired and then take a look at it and actually write the posts you've planned when inspiration is running a little low.

You have many ways to keep an editorial calendar. You could use a spread-sheet or your computer's calendar program (perhaps using Outlook if you're on a PC or iCal on a Mac). There's even a free plug-in for WordPress that allows you to organize your posts in a calendar within the admin interface. You can get the plug-in, cleverly named Editorial Calendar, by downloading it from the WordPress Plugin Directory (http://wordpress.org/extend/plugins/editorial-calendar) or by searching in the Plugins section of the admin interface. (Chapter 14 covers how to find, install, and use plug-ins.)

Community

The best way to get people to read your blog is to read *their* blogs and interact with them. Leave comments, and link to blog posts you enjoy. After a while, you'll notice that other bloggers are returning the favor, and they'll tell two friends...who'll tell two of *their* friends. You get the idea.

Know your readers

You should also be sure to engage your readers in comments on your posts. People who leave comments generally fall into two categories:

- Your biggest fans

- Your biggest critics

Both groups, oddly enough, have strong opinions and are worth engaging. When a commenter gets a reply in a comment from the blog's author (or even a personal email), it makes him feel good.

 note   **Engaging with commenters requires balance, because not every comment requires a response. You'll need to decide for yourself how to determine when to respond and when not to.**

Take advantage of social media

At one time, blogging encompassed all that social media had to offer. Now, with the advent of Facebook, Twitter, and a host of other social-networking sites, blogging is just one star in the social-media constellation. This fact creates an opportunity for you to leverage your blog content on social-media sites.

Why not create a Twitter account for your blog? Several plug-ins will automatically tweet out links to new blog posts, and you can even use your blog-specific account to tweet with other people who are interested in the subject that you blog about. Then people will start following you on Twitter and find their way to your blog.

The kids, they love Facebook. Heck, my mom loves Facebook, and she isn't a big fan of technology in general (she'll never read this book, for example), which gives you an idea of how pervasive Facebook is. Chances are that most of the people reading your blog also use Facebook, so why not give them another way to follow your work?

You can set up a page for your blog on Facebook, which will allow people to "like" your blog. Depending on how you set things up, when someone likes you, she'll be able to read your blog's Wall on Facebook. (If you aren't familiar with Facebook, the Wall is an area of a Facebook account where people can leave comments and where the account owner can post links or comments of his own.) Several Facebook-related plug-ins can post your blog's content on your Facebook Wall, which then allows people to share it with their friends on Facebook.

 A word of warning: People expect a lot of engagement from Facebook, even more so than they do from blogs. I'm not exactly sure why that is, but if you decide to go the Facebook route, make sure that you set aside enough time to devote to your Facebook readers, some of whom will read your blog only via Facebook.

Final Thought

As I say at the start of this chapter, blogging is what you make of it. The most important thing to keep in mind is that this stuff is supposed to be fun. Sure, you have to put a lot of time and energy into a blog if you want it to be successful, but that's true of anything.

Now stop reading this book, and blog about something!

Index

Meet Creative Edge.

A new resource of unlimited books, videos and tutorials for creatives from the world's leading experts.

Creative Edge is your one stop for inspiration, answers to technical questions and ways to stay at the top of your game so you can focus on what you do best—being creative.

All for only $24.99 per month for access—any day any time you need it.